Cambridge Elements

Elements in Leadership
edited by
Ronald E. Riggio
Claremont McKenna College
Susan E. Murphy
University of Edinburgh
Founding Editor
Georgia Sorenson
University of Cambridge

SHARED LEADERSHIP 2.0

Taking Stock and Looking Forward

Christina L. Wassenaar
University of South Alabama
Craig L. Pearce
Pennsylvania State University
Natalia Lorinkova
Pennsylvania State University

Shaftesbury Road, Cambridge CB2 8EA, United Kingdom

One Liberty Plaza, 20th Floor, New York, NY 10006, USA

477 Williamstown Road, Port Melbourne, VIC 3207, Australia

314–321, 3rd Floor, Plot 3, Splendor Forum, Jasola District Centre, New Delhi – 110025, India

103 Penang Road, #05–06/07, Visioncrest Commercial, Singapore 238467

Cambridge University Press is part of Cambridge University Press & Assessment, a department of the University of Cambridge.

We share the University's mission to contribute to society through the pursuit of education, learning and research at the highest international levels of excellence.

www.cambridge.org
Information on this title: www.cambridge.org/9781009560511
DOI: 10.1017/9781009560467

© Christina L. Wassenaar, Craig L. Pearce and Natalia Lorinkova 2025

This publication is in copyright. Subject to statutory exception and to the provisions of relevant collective licensing agreements, with the exception of the Creative Commons version the link for which is provided below, no reproduction of any part may take place without the written permission of Cambridge University Press & Assessment.

An online version of this work is published at doi.org/10.1017/9781009560467 under a Creative Commons Open Access license CC-BY-NC 4.0 which permits re-use, distribution and reproduction in any medium for non-commercial purposes providing appropriate credit to the original work is given and any changes made are indicated. To view a copy of this license visit https://creativecommons.org/licenses/by-nc/4.0

When citing this work, please include a reference to the DOI 10.1017/9781009560467

First published 2025

A catalogue record for this publication is available from the British Library

ISBN 978-1-009-56051-1 Hardback
ISBN 978-1-009-56048-1 Paperback
ISSN 2631-7796 (online)
ISSN 2631-7788 (print)

Cambridge University Press & Assessment has no responsibility for the persistence or accuracy of URLs for external or third-party internet websites referred to in this publication and does not guarantee that any content on such websites is, or will remain, accurate or appropriate.

Shared Leadership 2.0

Taking Stock and Looking Forward

Elements in Leadership

DOI: 10.1017/9781009560467
First published online: March 2025

Christina L. Wassenaar
University of South Alabama

Craig L. Pearce
Pennsylvania State University

Natalia Lorinkova
Pennsylvania State University

Author for correspondence: Christina L. Wassenaar, Christina.L.Wassenaar@gmail.com

Abstract: Shared leadership entails a dynamic, interactive influence process among groups and teams. Whereas traditional models of leadership emphasize the importance of vertical leadership as a role occupied by an individual in a designated position, shared leadership emphasizes the importance of leadership as an unfolding social process, shifting the influence to the person with the most relevant knowledge, skills and abilities, juxtaposed against the emerging task-related requirements. Research shows that shared leadership is a robust predictor of group, team, and organizational outcomes across a variety of organizations, industries, and cultural contexts. In fact, shared leadership is a better predictor of outcomes than vertical leadership. This Element provides a comprehensive review of the research on shared leadership, and points to promising directions for the future, in terms of both research and the practical application of shared leadership in action. This title is also available as Open Access on Cambridge Core.

Keywords: leadership, shared leadership, team, teamwork, collaboration

© Christina L. Wassenaar, Craig L. Pearce and Natalia Lorinkova 2025

ISBNs: 9781009560511 (HB), 9781009560481 (PB), 9781009560467 (OC)
ISSNs: 2631-7796 (online), 2631-7788 (print)

Contents

1 Bringing Shared Leadership to the Fore — 1

2 Historical Bases of Shared Leadership — 10

3 Antecedents of Shared Leadership — 20

4 Outcomes of Shared Leadership — 29

5 Shared Leadership: A Future Research Agenda — 46

6 Putting Shared Leadership into Practice — 57

7 The Future of Shared Leadership — 63

   References — 69

1 Bringing Shared Leadership to the Fore

The discussion of leadership is omnipresent – of that there is no doubt. Leadership permeates every aspect of our lives, whether we like it or not. But what do we mean when we talk about leadership? Typically, the idea of leadership boils down to the exertion of some type of influence of one person on another person or on a group. For most people the idea of leadership conjures an image of a powerful person projecting influence downward, through an organizational or social hierarchy, onto others designated as followers or subordinates. Figure 1 captures the essence of this perspective on leadership. This weighted view of leadership – usually based on formal, hierarchical position – is generally termed vertical leadership or hierarchical leadership. While this is a very useful way to frame leadership, it is insufficient, at best, and neglects to encompass the vast array of nuance that is part of the enactment of influence between social actors.

Leadership is not just about a hierarchical position; it is not simply a role to play, a position to fill. In fact, many people can be put into formal positions of leadership but not really engage in much actual influence, other than through the administrative power that rests in their position. Their position becomes the mechanism for leadership, not the person. In contrast, there are some people who, while they do not occupy formal leadership positions, can often, through collaborative efforts, be highly influential, possibly enabling entire social movements, changing the course of history (see Pearce & van Knippenberg, 2023 for a discussion of the leadership of social innovation). This informal perspective on leadership is generally termed shared leadership, where multiple people rise to the challenge and lead one another.

This book will focus on shared leadership – leadership from informal sources – especially as it relates to the leadership of groups, teams, and organizations. We will explore it as both an informal, naturally occurring phenomenon, but also discuss how to enable more leadership to be shared through intentional, thoughtful decisions on the part of the formal leader, as well as the organizations in which they work. Shared leadership is generally defined "as a dynamic, interactive influence process among individuals in groups for which the objective is to lead one another to the achievement of group or organizational goals or both" (Pearce & Conger, 2003: 1). Pearce and Conger (2003) proffered that vertical leadership was part of the shared leadership process but also suggested that it would be useful to accord it unique status in the analysis of leadership processes. We come back to this issue in Section 5, where we discuss future research directions.

Figure 1 Traditional perspective on top-down leadership as a role

Today most people think of shared leadership as a normal part of the leadership lexicon. The reality, however, is that a clear definition, and thus the scientific study of shared leadership, has only been around for a few decades (Pearce & Conger, 2003). While it is now an established theoretical perspective used to guide scholarly inquiry into the topic, and as a framework to facilitate practitioner quests to improve organizations, the start of the field was rocky – the first major empirical article on shared leadership, by Pearce and Sims (2002), which is now cited more than 2,100 times, was initially met with much significant resistance by the gate keepers of the premier journals of the field. The idea was simply too far from the traditionally accepted norms where the vertical/formal leader held primacy as the main target of study, yet, in reality, sharing leadership has been part of human organizational experience for millennia.

This first study was rejected by most of the major journals in management, applied psychology, and leadership (*Academy of Management Journal, Administrative Science Quarterly, Journal of Applied Psychology, Personnel Psychology*, and *Leadership Quarterly*). It ultimately found a home in *Group Dynamics*, a newer journal, started in 1997 – and thus at the time not nearly as prestigious as the old guard publications – with a focus on small group research and innovation in the field. Yet, even the publishing process at *Group Dynamics* was not without its hurdles, requiring a challenging set of four rounds of revisions, and a change of editors, before the final acceptance. Over the years, many people have asked why we didn't publish that article in a "premier" journal, including the more recent editors of *Academy of Management Journal, Journal of Applied Psychology, Administrative Science Quarterly*, and *Personnel Psychology*. Our answer has always simply been that we tried … but new thought does not always meet with the formal leader's (in this case, the leading journals' editors) approval, as they would be required to shift their mindset away from established norms regarding the *source of influence*.

It took six years from initial submission of the original Pearce and Sims manuscript to a journal for it to be published in 2002. At the time, the manuscript simply did not fit the predominant paradigm of top-down, vertical leadership. The editors of these journals, at the time, were uniformly encouraging of the novel aspects of the manuscript but, likewise, uniformly concerned that the construct of shared leadership simply was not leadership – they wished us luck in publishing elsewhere and chose to stay embedded in the idea that leadership influence was *not* a bilateral experience, much less, multidirectional – as we now clearly know it is.

Nonetheless, some form of shared leadership has been practiced in many groups and societies for as long as humans have engaged in complex, social, and creative activities, requiring divergent inputs from diverse individuals to develop breakthrough solutions to intractable problems. For example, the ancient Greeks devised an early system of democracy in an effort to decentralize power and to enable leadership from a broader group of people than was possible under the traditional approach to top-down leadership inherent in a hereditary monarchy. They recognized the latent issues that come with embedding leadership through an accident of birth and created deliberate structures to allow for a shared voice in leading their society. Almost a thousand years later, the Anglo-Saxons developed a structure where their kings were elected through an Assembly, sometimes called the *Witenagemot* – a group of secular and ecclesiastic delegates – who were then expected to advise the king on policies and laws, based on their personal expertise. The essence of this society was that it was organized with the understanding that influence between the king and assembly was reciprocal, and mutually reliant. This governance structure ended abruptly in 1066 with the Norman invasion and the reversion to the Frankish norms of hereditary kingship, but the people of Britain never quite lost their desire for sharing the lead – hence their rebellion, which culminated in the publication of the *Magna Carta* in 1215.

In a similar vein, Mandela, in his autobiography, wrote that the core tenets of his leadership style were formulated from watching how his tribal leader would sit silently as his people talked, listening to them, hearing their thoughts and needs, seeing the dynamics that were employed to develop a more complete and complex understanding of a situation, after which, the chief would summarize the discussion, noting where ideas had emerged from, as a mechanism to acknowledge and reward the influence that had been exerted by the various tribal members.

People want to share the lead. It's not that we don't recognize that it's useful to have someone to whom we can point at and say that they are responsible, but it is also in our nature to want to be heard, seen, and valued for our ideas and to be acknowledged as influential. With that said, we will focus this Element on the scientific side of the shared leadership equation, illuminating the progress made to date, as well as articulating promising avenues for future inquiry.

Pearce and colleagues (e.g., Pearce, 1993, 1995, 1997; Pearce & Sims, 2000, 2002; Pearce & Conger, 2003) are credited as the pioneers in crafting the shared leadership space, especially the Pearce and Sims (2002) empirical article on the relative influence of vertical versus shared leadership on team outcomes and the Pearce and Conger (2003) book which contained essays on shared leadership from the leading authorities on leadership and teamwork. These two publications are considered the seminal works on shared leadership, marking an inflection point and providing the catalyst for the increasing interest, in the ensuring years, in shared leadership. Since 2000, at least 1,225 articles and book chapters on shared leadership have been published in the scientific literature (see Figure 2). What is evident from the graph is that interest in shared leadership theory is on the rise.

Shared leadership is a philosophical perspective on leadership – with a foundational premise that nearly every single person is capable of leading, at least some of the time. This flies in the face of traditional notions of leadership – that leadership is something inherently special and few people are capable of being leaders. The more traditional concept of leadership has its roots, scientifically, in the "great man" philosophy, suggesting that leaders are rare, and that they are highly unique individuals with natural leadership abilities, and who should then be put into unilateral positions of power to exert downward influence on others, that is, vertical leadership.

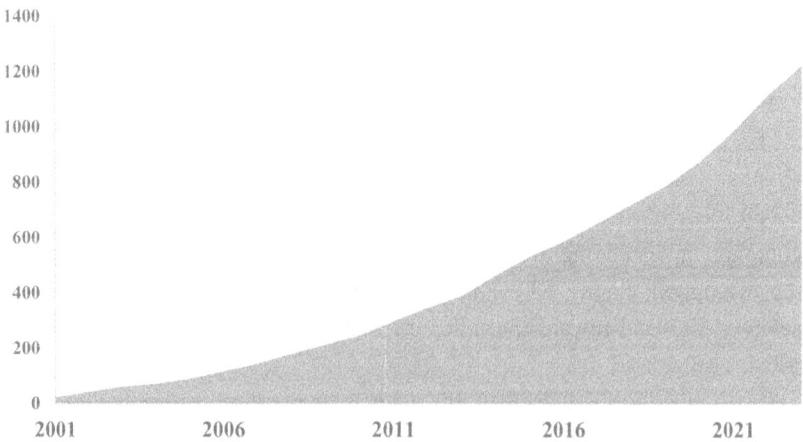

Figure 2 Cumulative research publications on shared leadership (2001–2023)

While we certainly do not subscribe to the "leadership is rare" ideology, we believe that top-down, vertical leadership is necessary in most human endeavors (see Pearce, 2004; Pearce, van Knippenberg, & van Ginkel, 2023 for a deeper discussion on this issue). We temper this perspective, greatly, however, by also advocating that shared leadership is necessary and, in fact, natural in those same endeavors as evidenced by the unintentional development of shared leadership structures throughout known human history.

With the uptick in interest regarding shared leadership as an area of research has been a proliferation of terms used to capture the notion of shared leadership – terms like *collective leadership*, *distributed leadership*, and many others. While we applaud the interest in the space, we caution against this proliferation of terms in both the academic and also in the practitioner literatures as it dis-unifies the definitional discussion for no clear theoretical gain. It typically causes more confusion than it clears up and ends up creating organizational frustration due to missed or misguided expectations. While we believe that this confusion is generally unintentional, it is nevertheless distracting from the value of truly understanding shared leadership. From an individual researcher point of view, however, it is easy to understand how these terms are forwarded – these researchers are attempting to carve out an area of research that becomes associated with their name. Conger and Pearce (2003), in an effort to stimulate interest in shared leadership, likely hold a bit of the blame for this proliferation by specifically encouraging "academic entrepreneurism" in the field.

Nevertheless, to establish some order to this burgeoning area, Pearce, Manz, and Sims (2014) provided a framework for understanding the interrelationship of these various terms – identifying special cases of the overarching term of shared leadership: rotated shared leadership, integrated shared leadership, distributed shared leadership, and comprehensive shared leadership (see Figure 3). One could easily identify additional special cases of shared leadership to add to this list (e.g., dyadic shared leadership). Nonetheless, the upshot is that all of these interrelated terms are, in the end, shared leadership. The field would do better to rationalize these terms into the overarching umbrella term of shared leadership, while continuing to explore such special cases. Otherwise, to simply proliferate terms in order to attempt to put a scholarly stake in the ground creates more confusion than it clarifies when it comes to the science of shared leadership.

Notwithstanding the special case of what is termed self-leadership (Manz, 1986), the generally understood term of leadership focuses on influence processes *between* people – that is, a leader who influences and a follower who accepts, influence. Historically, the scientific study of leadership has focused on one part of this equation, that is, just the top-down influence of a designated or

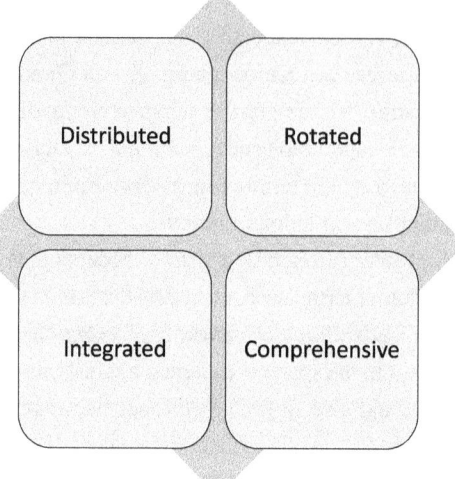

Figure 3 Primary forms of shared leadership

appointed leader on someone or some group of people below that person. Nonetheless, even in such circumstances there are almost always additional influence factors in the social situation that are not captured by studying leadership with that singular lens. Shared leadership research addresses this gap and provides a more encompassing view of leadership social dynamics. Leadership implies the existence of influence between people. Shared leadership is an overarching term that encapsulates all leadership social influence: all leadership is shared leadership; it is simply a matter of degree.

Perhaps now, as a continued remedy to this definitional proliferation and concept blur, it would be more useful to conceptualize shared leadership as a meta-theory. Calling it this does not assume that shared leadership assumes primacy or a higher level of importance than other theoretical work on leadership; we believe that calling it this is more of a clarifying description of a theory that can be described as something distinct, but that also permeates many other leadership, or influence based experiences. It is meta also in that shared leadership theory is integrative, or holistic in nature and, as we increasingly develop more sophistication in our models, especially now that so much ground work has been laid (see Sections 3 and 4), it is time to explore how shared leadership can both synthesize and unify varying leadership perspectives more seamlessly, ultimately with the goal of reflecting the organizational experience more accurately.

There are several primary dimensions along which leadership is shared. The first, of course, is reasonably straightforward and has to do with the number of people, from the social grouping of interest, involved in influencing one another. Second, we can ascertain the degree of influence the various actors have upon one another. This is also fairly straightforward. Third, we can consider the type of influence the various actors have which is a bit more complex than the first two dimensions. On the one hand, the type of influence might vary between people, which is natural. But, in a more overarching sense it is the range of types of influence that are important here. Figure 4 captures these three components, which comprise the degree of shared leadership inherent in situations.

Building on the previous dimensions, there are four fundamental types of leadership influence that can be exerted between people, ranging from directive to transactional, visionary and empowering (see Pearce et al., 2003 for a thorough discussion). The most common idea is that people would, based on their inclinations, enact the behaviors and attitudes associated with their dominant leadership style without any facility for shifting from one type to another. For example, the most obvious and typically understood type of influence is directive (sometimes referred to as authoritative) leadership. This entails providing instruction and commands to others, and assigning goals and similarly aligned influence strategies. Transactional leadership influence is focused upon setting up reward contingencies for desired outcomes, that is, providing rewards, either material, such as monetary rewards, or more personal rewards, such as recognition and praise, to induce others to engage in a course of action. Visionary leadership is more overarching and long-term oriented (of course visionary leadership is related to the term *transformational leadership*, but see van Knippenberg and Sitkin (2013) for a comprehensive discussion on the scientific issues surrounding transformational leadership). This type of

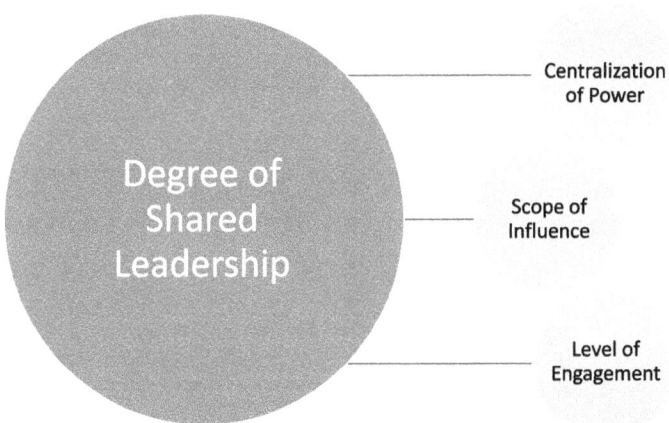

Figure 4 Underlying dimensions related to the degree of shared leadership

influence is focused on aligning others toward an overarching mission or toward some type of idealized state for the future. Finally, empowering leadership influence processes are focused on developing and unleashing the leadership capabilities of others. Figure 5 illustrates the scientific backdrop of these four encompassing types of leadership behavior and Figure 6 details the more precise components of each type, specifying the application and potential pitfalls of each influence strategy.

Shared leadership, however, is not just about types of influence behaviors, in isolation. The core dynamics of shared leadership center on shared leadership cognition, shared leadership learning, and shared leadership behavior (van Knippenberg, Pearce & van Ginkel, 2024). Shared leadership cognition entails mental models people hold when it comes to the enactment of leadership influence processes in social interactions – what they believe to be appropriate ways to engage in influence. Shared leadership learning involves the processes involved in refining shared leadership cognition, in line with training and development, as well as experience and reflection. Shared leadership behavior entails the actual engagement in social influence between social actors and may involve any or all of the various types of influence identified and described in Figure 6, that is, directive, transactional, visionary and empowering leader behaviors. We assert that these three constructs, in concert, form the core dynamics of shared leadership. We elaborate on this assertion in Section 5.

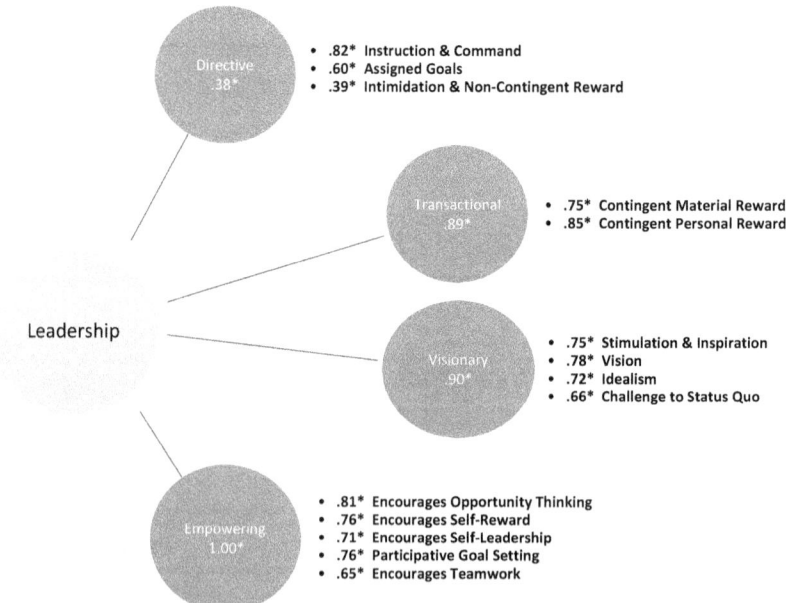

Figure 5 Fundamental leadership influence strategies

Leader Behavior	When to Deploy	Potential Liabilities
Directive	❏ When individuals are new ❏ When others are not skilled at the task ❏ For immediate actions (e.g., the building is on fire)	❏ Limits development of followers ❏ Places large burden on the leader ❏ Limits amount of information considered
Transactional	❏ Rational maintenance leadership ❏ For exemplary performance ❏ For social celebration of contributions	❏ Creates over emphasis on "extrinsic" motivation ❏ Narrows focus of followers work to those things that are explicitly rewarded
Visionary	❏ Provides focus on overarching goals ❏ Enables people to fill in the blanks between specific tasks ❏ Encourages citizenship behavior ❏ Facilitates resilience in the face of setbacks	❏ Is confounded with narcissism—followers need to be careful to evaluate the sincerity of the leader ❏ Can grow tiresome if overdone for trivial tasks
Empowering	❏ Is focused on development of others ❏ Creates higher levels of ownership ❏ Creates higher levels of motivation ❏ Creates higher levels of commitment	❏ Often leaders empower others without clearly specifying boundaries—boundaries must be clear ❏ People must be capable and responsible with empowerment—not everyone can be trusted to receive empowerment

Figure 6 Deployment and caveats regarding fundamental leadership influence strategies

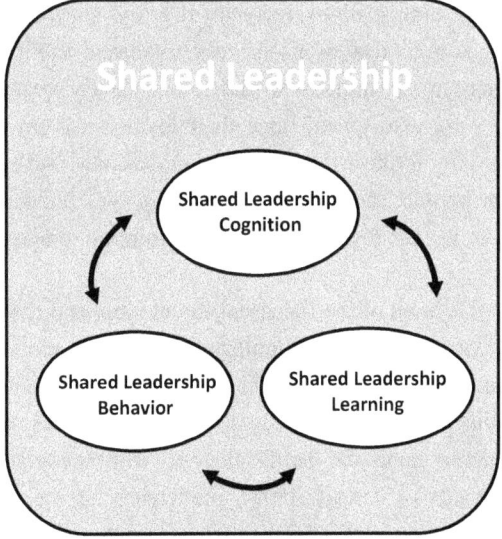

Figure 7 The core dynamics of shared leadership

In the following sections we first provide an analysis of the historical foundations of shared leadership in the management, organizational behavior, and applied psychology literatures. Then, we provide a comprehensive review of the scientific progress on shared leadership, exploring both the antecedents and outcomes of shared leadership. Subsequently, we turn our attention to highlighting the key avenues for future research, clarifying the progress to date in seven research domains relating to shared leadership (Conger & Pearce, 2003). Next, we proffer advice regarding the practice of shared leadership. Finally, we provide some concluding thoughts on the current state of the field.

2 Historical Bases of Shared Leadership

Prior to the Industrial Revolution, very little intellectual effort was given to the scientific study of leadership. That is not to say that people were not interested in leaders and their sources of influence; it is just that the attempt to evaluate that influence using some sort of scientific method was essentially nonexistent. Still, a great deal about leadership philosophy can be gleaned from the writings of Cicero, or from Machiavelli, who, in his both famous and oftreviled book *The Prince*, offered leadership advice to hereditary princes and church leaders, but also to a new sort of prince, as he called them – people who we would now call business leaders.

Looking further east, Saladin successfully navigated his rise to leadership between three contentious and competitive empires (Damascus, Baghdad, and Egypt) to build an almost obsessively loyal army, capable of defeating the Crusader armies. A great deal of his success was based on his patient development of a system of trusted aides, who understood clearly what the overall goals were, and who were also given, once their loyalty was proven, an unusual measure of autonomy for how they achieved those goals. Yet even with each of these significant people, the study of leadership was almost always merely anecdotal – that is, until the Industrial Revolution emerged as a global phenomenon.

It was during the dawn of the Industrial Revolution, and more specifically in the late 1700s, we witness the beginnings of the application of the scientific process to all manner of issues that could be converted into productive economic endeavors (Nardinelli, 2008). Naturally, the vast majority of these early efforts were more centered upon the hard sciences, with the goal of developing technological advances (Stewart, 1998), particularly as the role of people in the Industrial Revolution were mainly seen as supplementary to the far more interesting mechanical opportunities for the time. With that said, Stewart (2003) noted that by the end of the eighteenth century many of those who were considered scientists also began to address the questions related to the measurement of the social and managerial issues involved in organizational activities. There were people like Jean-Jacques Rousseau, who, in 1762, wrote *The Social Contract* (for a translated edition of this work see Rousseau, 2018). At the time of publication, his work was deeply uncomfortable to many – where he argued against the idea of the hereditary top-down leader, instead advocating for rule "by the people." He also realized that the scientific focus on technical innovation only offered part of the answer to increased organizational efficiencies, and called for a more holistic focus on the impact of this growth on the humans who were instrumental in this revolution.

At the beginning of the nineteenth century, the French economist Jean Baptiste Say (1803/1964) observed that entrepreneurs "must possess the art of superintendence and administration" (p. 330). Economists, prior to his writing, were largely concerned with land and labor and, to some extent, capital as the important factors of production. Jean Baptiste Say's initial observations on entrepreneurship catalyzed interest into managerial insights for economic enterprise. Thus, early observations in this space were largely focused on what we would call the command-and-control model of hierarchical leadership (Pearce & Conger, 2003). It was much later in the nineteenth century that minor hints of the concept of shared leadership could be detected in management writing as an alternative approach to leading groups of people (Pearce & Conger, 2003). One such reason that the focus was so heavily on the top-down model of leadership was simply that human interaction was considered the province of the sociologists, theologians, and philosophers – which, given the fact that humans are at the core of all organizational interaction and innovation, is an extraordinarily narrow intellectual path. Yet, until quite recently, leadership in organizations was the province of economists, and leadership in societies was for the aptly named humanities to interpret.

Thus, in order to gain a more clear understanding of how the nineteenth century perceived the human side of organizations, it is useful to consider the work of people such as Durkheim (1893), who compared leadership emergence in the social structures to two different types of societies: one, where the innate sameness (e.g., shared kinship, history, interdependence, homogeneity, collective responsibility/goals) of the group resulted in the selection of a leader who embodied their own selves; the second, where what he labeled "organic solidarity" as a more dominant form of organizing and where leaders emerge more typically from merit and their demonstrated expertise. This second type of society is characterized by "a system of different organs each of which has a special role, and which are themselves formed of differentiated parts. Not only are social elements not of the same nature, but they are not arranged in the same manner" (cited from Durkheim

1973 translation, pg. 69). He goes on to describe that in this society, there *is* a moderating/central "organ" but that the rest of the group is coordinated and subordinated both to the central node but also to each other in a web of interdependence. In this society individuals are grouped by the nature of the activity that they contribute to the society – that is, an occupational expertise is necessary to participate in this society, and the amount of expertise and usefulness is how influence is gained, rather than from to whom one is born.

One of the more holistic and thus also pioneering thinkers of the nineteenth century, regarding systematic and integrative approaches to management and leadership, was Daniel C. McCallum. He developed what could be considered the first documented principles of management and leadership that could be widely applied across organizations and industries. One of the principles he articulated focused upon the importance of "unity of command," where orders originated from the top and were implemented by those at lower levels of the hierarchy (Wren, 1994). The overwhelming majority of writing about leadership during the Industrial Revolution focused on this top-down, command-and-control perspective (e.g., Montgomery, 1836, 1840). This command-and-control perspective became the globally acknowledged *de facto* model of leadership advice of the nineteenth century (Wren, 1994).

By the turn of the twentieth century the top-down model of leadership was firmly embedded in what became known as "scientific management" (Gantt, 1916; Gilbreth, 1912; Gilbreth & Gilbreth, 1917; Taylor, 1903, 1911). However, moving forward into the twentieth century, multiple ideas began to emerge that form the foundation for shared leadership. We identify twenty-four such concepts. These ideas are summarized in Table 1.

Figure 8 provides a graphic representation of how the twenty-four precursor ideas of shared leadership emerged through the decades. Moreover, the figure parses and categorizes these ideas by group-level issues versus individual-level issues. Ten of these foundational concepts were developed at the individual-level of analysis, while fourteen were generated at the group-level of analysis. In the following paragraphs we briefly review each of these ideas, associating them with their primary proponents.

Leadership Thinking of the Early Twentieth Century Related to Shared Leadership

While several of the most influential authors of the early twentieth century (e.g., Gantt, 1916; Gilbreth, 1912; Gilbreth & Gilbreth, 1917; Taylor, 1903, 1911), proponents of scientific management, advocated for and clearly articulated top-down model of leadership, there were pockets of early shared leadership

Table 1 Historical contributions to the theoretical foundations of shared leadership theory

Theory/Research	Key Issues	Representative Authors
Law of the situation	*Let the situation, not the person, determine the "orders."*	Follett (1924)
Human relations	*One should pay attention to the social and psychological needs of employees.*	Mayo (1933); Bernard (1938)
Social systems perspective	*People in organizations are embedded in social systems, which, in turn, influence behavior.*	Turner (1933)
Role differentiation in groups	*Members of groups typically assume different types of roles.*	Benne & Sheats (1948)
Co-leadership – mentor protégé	*Concerns the division of the leadership role between two people – primarily research examines mentor and protégé relationships.*	Solomon, Loeffler & Frank (1953)
Social comparison	*People engage in social comparisons with one another.*	Festinger (1953)
Social exchange	*People exchange punishments and rewards in their social interactions*	Homans (1958)
Management by objectives	*Subordinates and superiors jointly set performance expectations.*	Drucker (1954)
Emergent leadership	*Leaders can "emerge" from a leaderless group.*	Hollander (1961)
Mutual leadership	*Leadership can come from peers.*	Bowers & Seashore (1966)
Expectation states theory	*Team members develop models of status*	Berger, Cohen & Zelditch (1972)

Table 1 (cont.)

Theory/Research	Key Issues	Representative Authors
	differential between various team members.	
Participative decision making	*Under certain circumstances, it is advisable to elicit more involvement by subordinates in the decision-making process.*	Vroom & Yetton (1973)
Vertical dyad linkage	*Examines the process between leaders and followers and the creation of in-groups and out-groups.*	Graen (1976)
Substitutes for leadership	*Situation characteristics (e.g., highly routinized work) diminish the need for leadership.*	Kerr & Jermier (1978)
Leader member exchange	*Examines the quality of exchanges between leaders and followers*	Liden & Graen (1979)
Self-management	*Given certain tools, employees, in general, can manage themselves.*	Manz & Sims (1980)
Self-leadership	*Employees, given certain conditions, are capable of leading themselves.*	Manz (1986)
Participative goal setting	*Examines how to set goals in participation with subordinates*	Erez & Arad (1986)
Self-managing work teams	*Team members can take on roles that were formerly reserved for managers.*	Manz & Sims (1987)
Followership	*Examines the characteristics of good followers.*	Kelly (1988)

Shared Leadership 2.0

Table 1 (cont.)

Theory/Research	Key Issues	Representative Authors
Empowerment	*Examines power sharing with subordinates.*	Conger & Kanungo (1988)
Team member exchange	*Examines how team members engage in social exchanges.*	Seers (1989)
Shared cognition	*Examines the extent to which team members share similar mental models about key internal and external environmental issues.*	Klimoski & Mohammed (1994); Cannon-Bowers, Salas & Converse (1993)
Co-leadership – role sharing	*Examines how two leaders can share a leadership role.*	Heenan & Bennis (1999)

Adapted from: Pearce and Conger (2003) Shared leadership: Reframing the hows and whys of leadership. Thousand Oaks, CA: Sage.

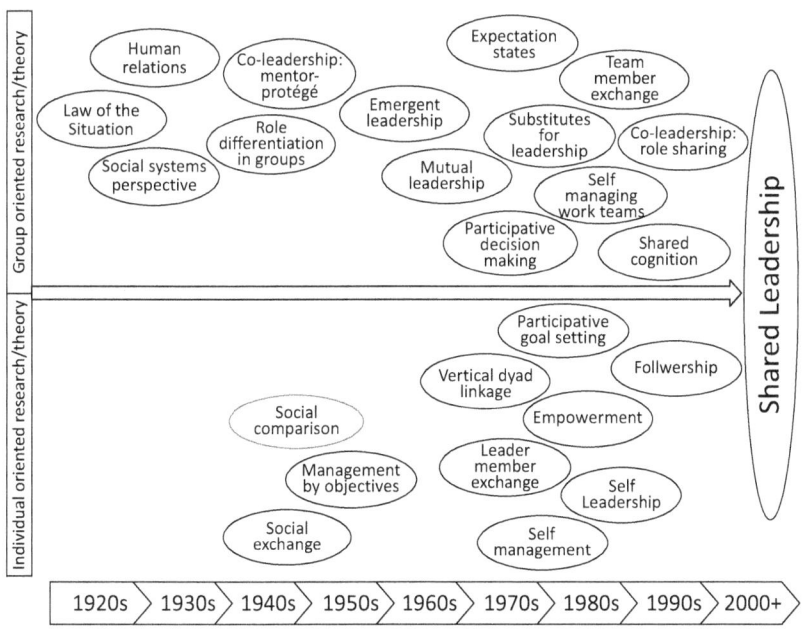

Figure 8 The shared leadership timeline: Foundations in theory and research.

discourse, even if it was not labeled as such. For instance, Mary Parker Follett, a community activist and management consultant, advocated a concept called the law of the situation (Follett, 1924). The essence of the law of the situation was that, instead of simply following the dictates of someone in a hierarchical position, people should take direction from the person with the most knowledge about the situation at hand, and that this would vary from situation to situation. At the time of publication, this was a novel idea and was in sharp contrast to the prevailing wisdom of the day when it came to leadership. Her perspective is clearly a forerunner of shared leadership theory.

Even though Follett was popular as both a management consultant and as a speaker in the 1920s, her thinking was largely discounted by the majority of the mainstream business community. One might speculate that the economic uncertainties of the time may have had a role in that regard. For instance, the world was filled with uncertainty with respect to the classic external organizational factors (i.e., political, economic, sociocultural, technological, legal, and environmental (PESTLE) (Aguilar, 1967), especially during the late 1920s through the mid 1940s, and this may have caused business leaders to loathe the notion of giving up control to others that was inherent in Parker's writings. With that said, Peter Drucker called her "the brightest star in the management firmament" in her era (Drucker, 1995, p. 2).

Regardless of the global systemic upheaval, in the 1930s, the human relations school (e.g., Bernard, 1938; Mayo, 1933) and social systems perspective (Turner, 1933) also both articulated the importance to paying attention to workers and that their psychological needs were imbedded in the social systems of economic activity. As such, these early writers foreshadowed the concept of shared leadership.

Mid Twentieth-Century Developments Related to Shared Leadership

As we move forward to the 1940s and 1950s, we note additional perspectives adding foundational work for the ultimate development of shared leadership theory. For example, Benne and Sheats (1948) described the notion of role differentiation in groups, where various members would have a role for influencing group achievement due to their experience and topical knowledge, as just two examples. Solomon, Loeffler, and Frank (1953) described the idea of "co-leadership" in mentor-protégé relationships in psychological counseling. They found that even if the therapeutic team were different in seniority in title, neither co-leader would be placed in a differing level of authority or dominance, while in the therapeutic group meeting setting and, in fact, they would behave as supportive partners who shared responsibility for a common goal.

Further, two theories elaborated on key social interactions: social comparison theory was articulated by Festinger (1953), where group members include ability evaluation in their assessment of others, and secondly, where the stability of that evaluative process is predicated on the similarities or divergences from the others' abilities, often compared to their own as 'prototypes', and social exchange theory as explained by Homans (1958) as the interaction that occurs when influence is gained from others by the act of accepting the other's influence in return. Finally, Drucker (1954) forwarded the concept of management by objectives, which described both the allowance and innate desirability for individuality in goal setting but also highlights how those individual goals exist in an interdependent organizational system – reinforcing the notion that organizations are essentially systemic communities of interdisciplinary actors reliant upon one another for success, rather than independent cogs or constituents. Each of these ideas from the 1940s and 1950s added additional intellectual components for the construction of shared leadership theory.

Building on this previous work, scholars in the 1960s provided additional insights closely aligned with shared leadership theory. For instance, Hollander (1961) observed and wrote about the idea of leader emergence from leaderless groups, while Bowers and Seashore (1966) observed what they called mutual leadership, where the support for a group's needs could be offered by the formal leader or members for each other, or both. These two concepts are core intellectual contributions to the ultimate development of shared leadership theory.

Late Twentieth-Century Thinking Related to Shared Leadership

In the 1970s we witnessed an accelerated pace of scientific discoveries related to shared leadership. For instance, Berger, Cohen and Zelditch (1972) postulated expectation states theory, that is, how individual expectation-states are formed and determine interactive behavior between members of a group. Group members form different evaluations of status, expectations of status, and, overall, generally different expectations based on the assessment of status characteristics. Vroom and Yetton (1973) articulated the idea of participative decision making, and Graen (1976) described the concept of vertical dyad linkage, which built on previous ideas about social exchange mechanisms. A bit later in the decade, Kerr and Jermier (1978) forwarded the notion of substitutes for leadership and Liden and Graen (1979) articulated the importance of leader-member exchange – that is, leaders will form relationships that differ with each of their followers/subordinates based on various factors, including leadership styles and subordinate roles. All of these concepts provide additional explicative foundations for shared leadership theory.

In the 1980s and 1990s we witnessed several additional developments regarding concepts related to shared leadership. For instance, Manz and Sims (1980) forwarded the notion of self-management, where group members managed their own behaviors by self-administering consequences for their performance, which Manz subsequently developed into the concept of self-leadership (Manz, 1986). Self-leadership expanded the previous work on self-management in that it explored the role of intentional self-influence (self-leading) on personal growth, motivation, and performance. Relatedly, Erez and Arad (1986) described the process of participative goal setting, where they found that cognitive, social, and motivational participation factors were useful in facilitating positive group and organizational outcomes. Finally, Manz and Sims (1987) investigated self-managing work teams and the seemingly paradoxical nature of a leader's role in such a team, and the behaviors that are useful to cultivate in facilitating a team where the leader becomes nominally superfluous yet still present.

Following in these footsteps, Kelly (1988) articulated the concept of followership, mainly in answer to the almost universal focus on the leader. He noted that if followers were considered, it was usually still simply to bring more clarity to the role of "leader," yet to exclude them as a discrete component of the relationship was to paint an incomplete picture of both, as neither exists without each other. Conger and Kanungo (1988) forwarded a model of the empowerment process that integrated the diverse viewpoints of the field from both the management and psychology literatures and Seers (1989) provided a perspective on team member exchange relationships that provided a complementary clarity of the role that quality team member exchange relationships played intra-team, thus rounding out the network relationships that were initially explored in the earlier leader-member exchange research.

Finally, the idea of shared cognition, also known as shared mental models, as illuminated by Cannon-Bowers, Salas and Converse (1993) as well as Klimoski and Mohammed (1994) are useful in understanding more of how teams make decisions, particularly with respect to how consequences are defined in the context of the team. Klimoski and Mohammed (1994) note that while Durkheim (1895/1938) also made mention of the idea "group mind," it was more to imply a general sense of unified collectiveness. However, the early interest in understanding this notion of individual group member's various expectations, thoughts, beliefs, and perceptions as a summative group-level phenomenon had fallen away until the later twentieth century when there was again critical interest in more purposeful exploration of the value not just in the top-down leader's vision-making process, but the notion of shared thought as organizationally beneficial. Slightly later, Heenan and Bennis (1999) described an alternative type of co-leadership that involved truly equal role sharing between two leaders, what they called *vertically contiguous* leaders who shared the leadership responsibilities of their respective positions. They elaborated further by highlighting that the truly "shrewd leaders of the future are those who recognize the significance of creating alliances with others whose fates are correlated with their own" (Heenan & Bennis, 1999: viii).

Summary of Twentieth-Century Intellectual Foundations of Shared Leadership

We have very briefly discussed some of the most important historical underpinnings to the development of shared leadership theory – from the Industrial Revolution, which began in Great Britain, but which quickly spread to the rest of the globe, to the pioneers in the area of scientific management, to several interesting and valuable streams of research that allow us more clarity for understanding the development of shared leadership theory.

While two of these earlier publications (Follett, 1924; Bowers & Seashore, 1966) might best be described as one-hit-wonders, which were squarely in line with shared leadership, they quickly faded from the scientific discourse. Clearly, the scientific community did not embrace these ideas at the time but they, nonetheless, provided important intellectual stakes in the ground for our current understanding of shared leadership theory. What *is* clear is that each of these scientific traditions provide intellectual ingredients for the galvanization of shared leadership theory, and again, reinforce that shared leadership theory exists in a meta theoretical plateau, in that it is woven from both supportive and contextual social experiences that when drawn together create an environment where shared leadership can exist.

It is always important to look back in time, to understand how we have arrived at our current location. The historical backdrop of shared leadership theory is rich and complex and up until quite recently, fragmented within other human social experience without much theoretical clarity. With that said, it is now uniformly understood that shared leadership is a critical frame through which to conceptualize leadership dynamics. To wit, in Section 1 we provided an overview graph documenting the rising interest in shared leadership, particularly from the early 2000s. From humble beginnings in the 1990s (Pearce, 1993, 1995, 1997) and two key publications (Pearce & Sims, 2002; Pearce & Conger, 2003) in the early 2000s, we now witness an exponential growth in the number of publications on shared leadership, both empirical and conceptual in nature, across many disciplines (e.g., organizational psychology, management and sociology, political science, etc.) and industry sectors (e.g., healthcare, education, public administration, engineering, construction, etc.). Since 2000, at least 1,225 research-focused publications have appeared on shared leadership, with many more in the popular literature, and the number and type of work in this area is not only accelerating in actual numbers but also in the sophistication of analysis. In the next two sections, we delve much more deeply into the research findings surrounding shared leadership.

3 Antecedents of Shared Leadership

Twenty years ago most of the literature regarding the antecedents of shared leadership was conceptual in nature (e.g., Burke, Fiore, & Salas, 2003; Ensley, Pearson, & Pearce, 2003; Houghton, Neck, & Manz, 2003; Mayo, Meindl, & Pastor, 2003; Pearce, 1993, 1995, 2004; Pearce & Conger, 2003; Pearce & Sims, 2000). Nonetheless, more recently there have been significant empirical advances in the study of factors that support the formation of shared leadership.

While antecedents of phenomena are critical to a scientific understanding, researchers typically examine outcomes more frequently than antecedents, and shared leadership is no exception. Thus, the predominance of empirical studies of shared leadership has focused on understanding the outcomes. With that said, some researchers have been focusing efforts on developing a richer and deeper understanding of the precursors of shared leadership in teams and organizations. In this vein, empirical research addressing the antecedents of shared leadership has primarily examined four fundamental types of antecedents: (1) vertical leadership, (2) organizational support systems and structures, (3) cultural context, and (4) team factors. Table 2 summarizes this research.

We do not purport that these categories represent a typology of potential antecedents of shared leadership but rather that they provide a useful organizing mechanism for reporting the results that have been found to date. Accordingly, we review each of these categories, in turn, in the following paragraphs, after that we subsequently discuss several research advances regarding antecedents of shared leadership which do not fall neatly into these categories.

Vertical Leadership

Much of the theoretical writing about antecedents of shared leadership has focused on the role of vertical leadership. This seems quite logical for two reasons: first, because the traditional focus in leadership research has been on the formal leaders, but second, and more importantly, the formal leader would

Table 2 Summary of current state of antecedent research on shared leadership

Vertical Leadership	Leader support/enabling resources/trust/transformational/transparency/vision/ empowering/humility/shared decision-making/servant leadership/engagement/ coaching/goal alignment/expectations of excellence/matching skills/creating focus/ feedback/freedom/safety/values alignment/responsibility/diversity orientation/ fairness/gender
Organizational Support Systems	Technology that supports collaboration/communication/institutional empowerment/selection/compensation/education, training and development/shared events/planned responsibility distribution/equity/shared cues/coaching
Cultural Context	Organizational cultural/group values/cultural structures/participative safety/voice/social support/purpose/intentional social structures/entrepreneurial support/proactivity/open feedback/autonomy/feedback/job characteristics/perceptions of empowerment/empowerment culture
Team Factors	Group member behaviors/complementary expertise/cohesive support/collective achievement/transactional knowledge/knowledge sharing/beliefs about competency and ability/task interdependence/goal interdependence/team connectedness/informal communication opportunities/extraversion/empathy/core self evaluations (CSE)/homogeneity/collective identification/team rewards/member integrity/voice/perceived virtuality/task reflexivity/expectations of creativity/work complexity

appear to be critical component of shared leadership emergence in a group or team. As such, it is not surprising that a great deal of the empirical work on antecedents of shared leadership has focused on this issue. For example, (Hoch, 2013; Hess, 2015) found vertical leader support (e.g., commitment to the team, continuous reinforcement of involvement and of team autonomy, and commitment to enabling resources) to be linked to shared leadership development. Moreover, George, Burke, Rodgers, Duthie, Hoffmann, Koceja et al. (2002),

Klasmeier and Rowold (2020), and Olson-Sanders (2006) identified trust in the vertical leader to be directly associated with shared leadership development.

More recently, in the context of police work, Masal (2015) found transformational leadership from above to be a predictor of shared leadership. Transformational leadership has been evaluated by others as well (e.g., Hoch, 2013; Klasmeier & Rowold, 2020; Tung & Shih, 2023; Von Stieglitz, 2023), with similar results.

Shamir and Lapidot (2003), in a study of the Israeli Defense Forces, concluded that goal alignment between leaders and followers, as well as follower trust in and satisfaction with vertical leaders, was associated with the development of shared leadership. Abson and Schofield (2022) found that a leader's transparency, and the development of a shared vision, was also integral for shared leadership to emerge in teams where knowledge work and high pressure was also present. This same research team, and others, have found that leaders who engage in empowering leadership behaviors will have followers who report more shared leadership (e.g., Carson, et al., 2007; Fausing, Joensson, Lewandowski, & Bligh, 2015, Grille, Schulte, and Kauffeld, 2015; Hoch, 2013; Lyndon, & Pandey, 2020; Margolis & Ziegert, 2016; Svensson, Jones, & Kang, 2021; Wassenaar, 2017).

In a similar vein, Elloy (2008) concluded vertical leader engagement with team members in decision-making facilitates the development of shared leadership, while more recently, several studies (e.g., Chiu, 2014; Chiu, Owens, & Tesluk, 2016; Svensson, et al., 2021) found that the humility demonstrated by the vertical leader to be a precursor of shared leadership, where humility promoted both leadership-claiming as well as leadership-granting behaviors from team members. Wang, Jiang, Liu, and Ma, (2017) and Svensson, et al., (2021) also found that servant leadership behaviors demonstrated by the leader led to more shared leadership in the sports teams that were the target respondents in their study, especially in development environments – that is, environments where the amount of resources are scant.

Hooker and Csikszentmihalyi (2003), in a qualitative study of research and development laboratories, found six vertical leader behaviors to provide the conditions for the development of shared leadership: (1) valuing excellence, (2) providing clear goals, (3) giving timely feedback, (4) matching challenges and skills, (5) diminishing distractions, and (6) creating freedom. Echoing some of these findings, Wood (2005) and Margolis and Ziegert (2016) found that leaders who enabled more group safety through lower levels of abusive supervision enable groups to experience more shared leadership. Similarly, in a series of qualitative studies, Pearce et al. (2014) found vertical leader engagement in empowering behavior, visionary behavior, as well as providing a focus on values to be associated with the development of shared leadership. Wassenaar (2017) found that a leader's diversity orientation and the perception of their fairness toward members of the team also resulted in higher levels of shared leadership.

While not directly associated with the formal leader of the team, Carson et al. (2007) noted that supportive coaching from external leaders – leaders who are not in any sort of supervisorial role of the team members – was useful in developing more shared leadership. Grille et al. (2015) note that team member's perception of how fairly they are rewarded by the leader, is also associated with shared leadership. Finally, in a study of several major Finnish healthcare organizations, Konu and Viitanen (2008) found that female vertical leaders are more likely to develop shared leadership than their male counterparts. In sum, these aforementioned studies identify a critical role of vertical leadership in the shared leadership equation.

Organizational Support Systems and Structures

A second major category of antecedents that have been linked to shared leadership are those that focus on support structures and systems within organizations. For example, information technology systems that facilitate collaboration continues to evolve in sophistication and scope, and where well used in organizations to develop communication and information exchange mechanisms for group work, has also been identified as a facilitator of shared leadership. To support this notion, Wassenaar, Pearce, Hoch, and Wegge (2010) found information technology support systems, in a qualitative study of German virtual teams, to facilitate the development of shared leadership. Similarly, Cordery, Soo, Kirkman, Rosen, and Mathieu (2009), in a study of parallel virtual global teams, found technological support structures, which focused on enabling team members to communicate more easily, and which facilitated the transfer of learning across team members, generated greater development of shared leadership across such teams.

Beyond technology, Pearce et al. (2014), in a compilation of qualitative studies, found that three key internal systems: selection; compensation; and education, training, and development systems were integral in providing a platform that enabled a shared leadership environment to evolve. The support of the organization for creating shared events, such as professional development opportunities or town hall meetings, as just two examples, are also useful platforms (Kang & Svensson, 2023). In that same study, Kang and Svensson (2023) also evaluated how strategic planning, in this case conceptualized as the strategic decision to distribute various leader functions collaboratively, resulted in reports of more shared leadership. Similarly, Hess (2015) found that focus on equity in team member recruitment and focus on team outcomes facilitated the development of shared leadership. Moreover, Elloy (2008), in a paper mill study, found team training, focused on collaborative communication, to be linked to the development of shared leadership. From a different perspective, DeRue, Nahrgang, and Ashford (2015) found perceptions of warmth (characterized by: benevolence, trustworthiness, and liking), and a shared understanding of network cues to be linked to the development of shared leadership.

A related line of inquiry that has gained traction in the literature is focused on the role of coaching (e.g., Bono, Purvanova, Towler, & Peterson, 2009; Leonard & Goff, 2003). In this regard, Carson et al. (2007), as well as Cordery et al. (2009), both found various forms of coaching to be positively linked to the demonstration and development of shared leadership. In total, organizational support systems and structures appear to be a critical ingredient when it comes to the development of shared leadership.

Cultural Context

While vertical leadership from above, as well as organizational support systems and structures have been linked to shared leadership development, another broad category of antecedents to shared leadership entails cultural context. Cultural context includes factors as broad as national and organizational culture, to shared team member values. Konu and Viitanen (2008), for example, identified team values as an important predictor of the development of shared leadership. Similarly, Carson et al. (2007), as well as Serban and Roberts (2016) and Wu, Cormican, and Chen (2020), as well as Carvalho, Sobral, and Mansur (2020), found what they labeled internal environments of groups, where there were higher levels of participative safety present, to be linked to the development of shared leadership (e.g., where environments that support shared voice, social support, and purpose). They found that this is where the internal culture of the team is intentionally set up to enable members to offer others leadership influence.

In a study conducted in innovation labs, Rose, Groeger, and Hölzle (2021) learned that cultivating a culture of shared voice, room for experimentation, and organized opportunities for entrepreneurial thinking resulted in shared leadership emergence in creative environments. Another consideration was uncovered by the team of Coun, Gelderman, and Perez-Arendsen (2015), where they were able to compare two different groups of people, both who experienced a New Ways of Working (NWW, facilitated by new and high levels of information communications technology) rollout in the organization, but where one group also had an articulated emphasis placed on support structures for proactivity. The assumption was that the NWW (characterized by an open feedback culture, more autonomy and internally supported entrepreneurship) would facilitate shared leadership emergence in both groups, but this was not the case, as the group that did have the proactivity support did report shared leadership, while the other group did not.

Wood (2005), in a study of church leadership, found that perceptions of empowerment by teams and their members were predictive of shared leadership behavior. Similarly, institutional empowerment has been linked to shared leadership (Mi et al., 2023). Finally, Pearce et al. (2014), across a number of qualitative studies, found organizational culture to be an important antecedent of shared leadership. Taken together, these studies point to an important role for cultural context as an important precursor of shared leadership.

Team Factors as Antecedents

Up until recently, the study related to antecedents included only the role that the vertical/formal leader played, organizational structures that help or harm, or cultural context factors in shared leadership emergence. However, there are now enough studies that have been done that a fourth category is needed – one that considers team factors separately. For example, Xu and Zhao (2023), in a mixed methods study, found that the macro level shared leadership phenomenon was enabled through individual team member behaviors (in their model they observed three dimensions: collective achievement leadership, cohesive support leadership, and complementary expertise leadership).

Transactional knowledge and knowledge sharing within and between team members have also emerged as important antecedents, as has been found in various studies (e.g., Abson, & Schofield, 2022; Fransen et al., 2018; Vandavasi et al., 2020). Fransen et al. (2018) also found that, in addition to their work on team transactional knowledge, the team members' beliefs about each other's competency, the perception of the other's ability to complete a task well, was an important factor for shared leadership. Similarly, Lyndon, Pandey, and Navare, (2022) found transactive memory systems to be positively related to shared leadership.

Another set of team-based antecedents are those related to the tasks that are expected from the team. Task interdependence, where team members are expected to rely on others' skills, interact with, and also depend on others to accomplish a goal (Guzzo & Shea, 1992), was found to be an antecedent of shared leadership in several studies (e.g., Fausing et al., 2015; Wu et al., 2020; Wu, Zhou, & Cormican, 2023). Fausing et al. (2015) note that they base their empirical work on Pearce and Sims' (2000) theoretical framework which highlighted the mutual cooperation, interaction, and guidance that is part of the shared leadership influence process, and also note that in contexts where interdependence is low, employees are also able to complete their work with less interaction with one another. This bears out the notion put forward by Wassenaar and Pearce (2012, p. 382) that "shared leadership is applicable only to tasks where there is interdependency between the individuals involved." Fausing et al. (2015) also found that goal interdependence, where the goals are specifically related to the work that is completed by the team itself and the members can see how their work fits into the completion of the whole, was a significant antecedent for shared leadership. Along this same vein, Hans and Gupta (2018) noted that the job characteristics of skill variety, task significance, autonomy, and feedback are significantly supportive of shared leadership, thus suggesting the notion that job design is a critical component for shared leadership.

Van Zyl (2020) found that team connectedness was a clear antecedent for shared leadership emergence in dispersed team members, but also notes that the type of interactions that generated the highest level of connectedness between these dispersed team members were informal connections made through shared interactions outside of formally organized settings. Building further on the type of team member interactions that are useful for shared leadership development, Ge et al. (2024) found that team-based relationship- and task-oriented personality compositions positively impact reported shared leadership when mediated by team member exchange (TMX). Further, Abson and Schofield (2022) note that empathy between the members in a team enhances the willingness for people to share influence among each other.

Team core self-evaluations (CSE) can also influence both the emergence and effectiveness (outcomes) of shared leadership (Siangchokyoo & Klinger, 2022). As an example, they note that the amount of homogeneity and team collective identification in team members CSE influence the decisions of team members to share leadership. Building on the notion of collective identification within teams, Gu, Hu, and Hempel (2022) found that the interdependence of team rewards and incentives positively supported more shared leadership in teams.

In an interesting study of both antecedents and outcomes of shared leadership, Hoch (2013) found that team member integrity was positively associated with shared leadership. Finally, Rose et al., 2021 noted that voice, where team members feel enabled "to speak up and get involved" (Carson et al., 2007, p. 1223), was positively related to how much shared leadership was reported in the respondents studied. This bears out the earlier findings from Carson et al. (2007), making voice an interesting factor to continue to study as part of shared leadership emergence. Darban (2022), in a university study with 341 students in

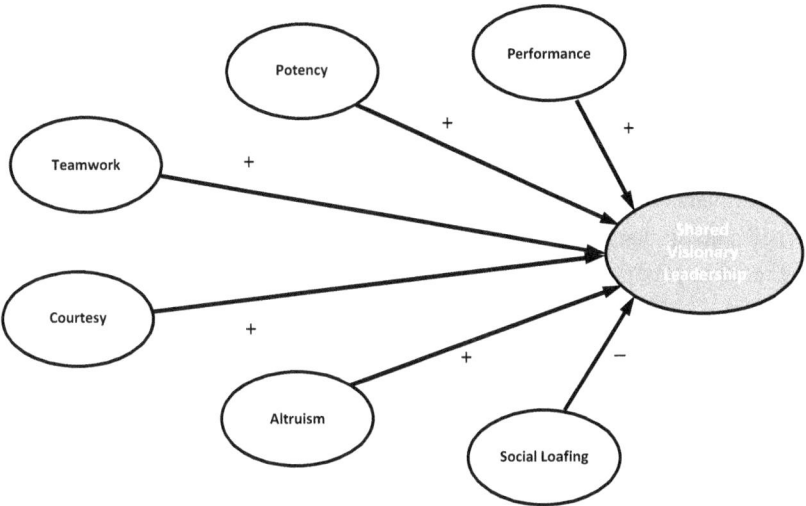

Figure 9 Antecedents of shared leadership in product and process improvement teams

48 virtual teams, found that team empowerment and perceived virtuality were positively associated with shared leadership, in turn increasing the team members intention to learn, and to update their knowledge about a topic.

Rose et al. (2021) note that the amount of shared leadership is also positively related to the team's expected creativity of the work output as well as the task reflexivity – how much the team members reflect on the goals and so on that are expected of them and feel willing and enabled to adapt them to current or expected circumstances (West, 1996). This idea particularly built on the theoretical work of Pearce (2004), where it was noted that where tasks were highly interdependent, complex, and requiring creativity, shared leadership would also be more likely to be present and useful. Finally, Pearce and Ensley (2004), in a study of product and process improvement teams, provided a fairly comprehensive analysis of antecedents of shared leadership. They identified prior team performance, team potency, teamwork, courtesy, and altruism as positive predictors of shared leadership, as well as social loafing as a negative predictor of shared leadership. Figure 9 provides a graphic view of this study.

Other Antecedents of Shared Leadership

Additional studies have examined factors that do not fall neatly into one of the above categories but have been linked to the development and display of shared leadership. Ropo and Sauer (2003), in a longitudinal study of orchestras, identified length of relationships between various members as an antecedent to shared leadership between orchestral constituents. Relatedly, Fransen et al., (2018) found that the amount of warmth-oriented traits (e.g., trustworthiness, helpfulness, and friendliness) that were exhibited by a team member are positively predictive of the amount of influence that team member would have in the group environment. Kang and Svensson (2023) noted that the personality traits of extraversion and introversion are important to the development of shared leadership, in that extraverts are more likely to share easily, and introverts can be more intentionally supported by the leaders and other team members.

From a different tack, Chiu (2014) found proactivity of team members to facilitate the development of shared leadership. Similarly, Pearce et al. (2014) found proactivity, trust, and openness to be related to the development of shared leadership, across a number of qualitative studies, while Hooker and Csikszentmihalyi (2003), in their study of research and development laboratories, identified the state of flow (Csikszentmihalyi, 1990) as a foundational link in the development of shared leadership. Moreover, Paunova and Lee (2016) found team learning orientation to be related to the development of shared leadership.

Muethel, Gehrlein, and Hoegl (2012), on the other hand, found demographic characteristics of groups affect the development of shared leadership. Kukenberger and I'Innocenzo (2020) note that certain types of diversity, such as gender diversity, will initially negatively impact the development of shared leadership, particularly in climates where cooperation is low, or the team is newly formed. However, as time passes, the impact of gender diversity will be mitigated, particularly in teams where task-related experiences are high. They also found that shared leadership was more present in teams who reported functional diversity *and* high levels of a cooperative climate. Serban and Roberts (2016) identified task cohesion as well as task ambiguity as factors related to shared leadership development. Finally, Hess (2015) found face-to-face teams to be more inclined to demonstrate and develop shared leadership than their virtual team counterparts. Together, these studies demonstrate a range of additional factors associated with the development of shared leadership.

Summary of the Empirical Examination of Antecedents of Shared Leadership

While there has lately been an increase in the number of studies (both qualitative and quantitative) on the antecedents of shared leadership, there are still far fewer relative to research on the outcomes of shared leadership. Nonetheless, given the clear value of shared leadership in many settings, there is a great deal of opportunity for more development in this area. Given this, we will specify some further possibilities for research on antecedents of shared leadership in Section 5. In the next section, however, we detail the work that has been done regarding the outcomes of shared leadership.

4 Outcomes of Shared Leadership

Much of the early work on the outcomes of shared leadership was conceptual in nature (e.g., Burke, Fiore, & Salas, 2003; Ensley, Pearson, & Pearce, 2003; Mayo, Meindl, & Pastor, 2003; Pearce, 1993, 1995; Pearce & Sims, 2000; Seibert, Sparrowe, & Liden, 2003) with emphasis placed on defining the concept of shared leadership and its role in the larger organizational literature. Over the last two decades, in addition to many qualitative investigations, the study of shared leadership has produced an increasingly wide and thoughtful body of quantitative studies that examine the relationship between shared leadership and a variety of outcomes. In fact, the proliferation of empirical research has allowed for the publication of no less than four different meta-analyses linking shared leadership to several important outcomes (Nicolaides et al., 2014; Wang et al., 2014; D'Innocenzo et al., 2016; Wu et al., 2020).

Research in organizational behavior generally references and studies outcomes at three different levels of analysis – individual-, group/team-, and organization-level outcomes, with shared leadership being no exception. Outcomes in organizational behavior and general management research include such things as cognition, attitudes, behavior, and performance. Some examples, at the individual-level of analysis, include individual job performance, job satisfaction, motivation, and well-being. Some examples of outcomes traditionally examined at the group/team level include group/team performance, collaboration and communication, coordination, team satisfaction, trust and cohesion, and similar concepts. Finally, some examples of organizational-level outcomes include such things as organizational financial performance, organizational culture and climate, customer service and satisfaction, and organizational turnover rate, to name a few.

By definition, shared leadership describes and refers to a group/team-level phenomenon; consequently, the majority of the empirical studies focus on group/team-level outcomes, although individual- and organizational-level outcomes have also been examined. Consequently, in the remainder of this section, we start with explaining the relationship between shared leadership and group/team outcomes, and then move on to briefly discuss individual and organizational level consequences of shared leadership.

Shared Leadership and Team-Level Outcomes

The examination of the team level consequences of shared leadership has been grounded in the general group/teams' research literature, which suggests that team effectiveness – an umbrella term defined in the section called shared leadership and overall team effectiveness – encompasses four categories: performance, attitudes, cognition, and behaviors (Cohen & Bailey, 1997; Cox, Pearce & Perry, 2003), with each one of these categories potentially subjected to the influence of shared leadership. Other authors (e.g., Nicolaides et al., 2014; Zhu et al., 2018; Pearce et al., 2023) split the consequences of shared leadership into proximal outcomes (e.g., team affective tone or team efficacy) and distal outcomes (e.g., team performance or team creativity), arguing that proximal outcomes transfer the influence shared leadership to, and, in turn, relate to distal outcomes. Both systematizations of the outcomes, however, may be traced back to the input-process-output model of team effectiveness (IPO), which we explain briefly in the next paragraph before we outline the specifics of the shared leadership outcomes.

Shared Leadership and Overall Team Effectiveness

As an umbrella term, *team effectiveness* encompasses performance as well as other team-level outcomes. Extant team effectiveness research dates to almost sixty years ago when McGrath (1964) advanced the so-called input-process-output (IPO) model for studying and analyzing the functioning of systems, including teams and organizations. This conceptual model breaks down a system into three main components – Inputs, Processes, and Outputs – and is often applied to the study and assessment of team effectiveness. Figure 10 contains a team context version of this model.

As represented by the figure and as noted by Mathieu and colleagues, in the IPO model "Inputs describe antecedent factors that enable and constrain members' interactions" (2008, p. 412). Inputs may be individual, such as individual team member characteristics (e.g., competence, personality); team, such as team task structure, team composition, or leadership, and contextual and organizational, such as environmental factors (e.g., external environment complexity or organizational factors, such as organizational climate or organizational structure). These inputs serve as antecedents for various processes, which describe members' interactions directed toward task accomplishment. Historically, team processes have been categorized as "taskwork" – or processes describing functions that team members engage in for team task accomplishment, and "teamwork" – or interactions between team members. In 2001, Marks and colleagues offered a new taxonomy, which discusses transition, action and interpersonal team

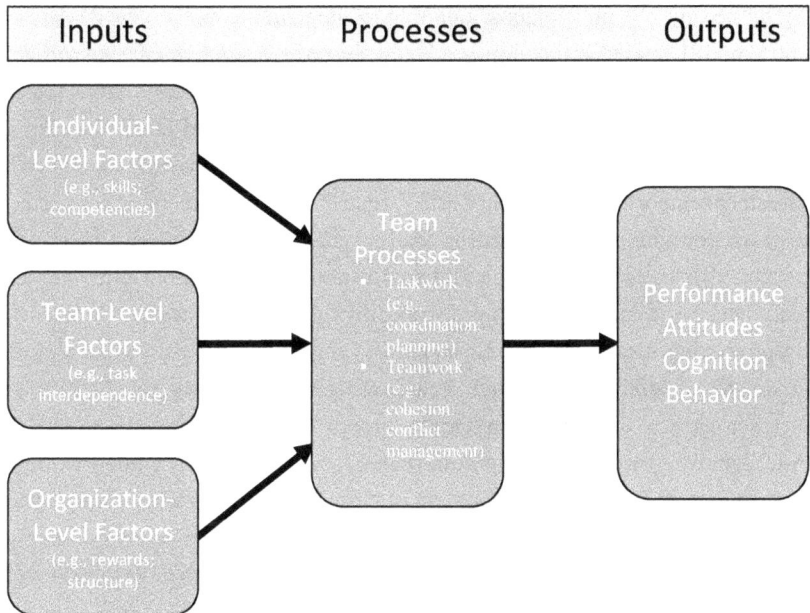

Figure 10 Input-process-output model of team effectiveness

processes, which have a more temporal nature and refer to planning and coordination activities, task-accomplishment related activities, and the more transient interpersonal processes, which include conflict management, trust building and similar interpersonal processes. Finally, outputs describe the results, outcomes, or products generated by the system, as a result of the processes applied to the inputs. In the context of teams, outputs can include the overall team performance, the achievement of the team's goals, or timely project completion. Outcomes, however, can also include more attitudinal, cognitive, or behavioral-based aspects such as increased knowledge, team members' cohesion, team vitality, and similar. In other words, "outcomes are results and by-products of team activity that are valued by one or more constituencies" (Mathieu et al., 2008). In the literature using the IPO model, leadership (including shared leadership) is usually treated as an antecedent factor (or input), and sometimes as a process, which influences several outputs. As seen from the figure and in the previous paragraphs, team effectiveness comprises both performance and other outcomes, with performance encompassing objective and subjective performance, and other outcomes encompassing team members' attitudinal (e.g., team members' overall satisfaction, commitment), cognitive (e.g., mental models) and behavioral outcomes (e.g., cooperation, helping and similar).

Defined as a "simultaneous, ongoing, mutual influential process" (Pearce 2004, p. 48), shared leadership is a leadership process that is enacted through social interactions among team members (Conger & Pearce, 2003), thus fostering positive outcomes for the team. For example, Hoch and Dulebohn (2013) advocate for improved decision-making process, whereas Bergman, Rentsch, Small, Davenport, and Bergman (2012) argue that shared leadership contributes to team cohesion, team consensus, and satisfaction through team members' improved knowledge exchange and motivation to take responsibility for the team success. Shared leadership also positively influences team effectiveness by promoting teamwork, shared mentality, and increased knowledge sharing among team members (e.g., Bligh, Pearce & Kohles, 2006; Erkutlu, 2012) and it also serves as a facilitator of effective group decision making (Hoch, 2013). Additionally, shared leadership contributes to the creation of a good working environment through the development of close relationships among employees (Hoch, 2013; Choi, Kim & Kang, 2017) because team members who interact closely and share leadership responsibilities are more likely to have lower levels of conflict and stress (Wood & Fields, 2007; Daspit et al., 2013).

Thus, research advocates for an overall positive relationship between shared leadership and overall team effectiveness. Perhaps the most comprehensive longitudinal empirical analysis of the relationship between shared leadership and effectiveness, Pearce and Ensley (2004) found a significant effect of shared leadership on team cognition, team behavior, and team performance (see Figure 11). In addition to many primary studies that find support for a direct positive relationship between shared leadership and team effectiveness (e.g., Choi, Kim, & Kang, 2017; Daspit Justice Tillman, Boyd, & Mckee, 2013; Pearce & Sims, 2002), this finding is supported by a number of meta-analytical investigations: Wang and colleagues (2014) report an overall effect size of $r = .29$ between shared leadership and team effectiveness, whereas Wu et al. (2020) who examine the relationship between shared leadership and what they call "overall outcomes", report an effect size of $r = .31$. As a result, researchers and practitioners alike commonly treat shared leadership as a positive antecedent of team effectiveness.

Moderators of Shared Leadership and Overall Team Effectiveness

Going one step further in examining the overall role of shared leadership in facilitating team effectiveness, a few authors also examine moderators of the shared leadership – team effectiveness relationship. For example, Hoch, Pearce, and Welzel (2010) found age diversity and coordination to moderate the relationship between shared leadership and team effectiveness.

Shared Leadership 2.0

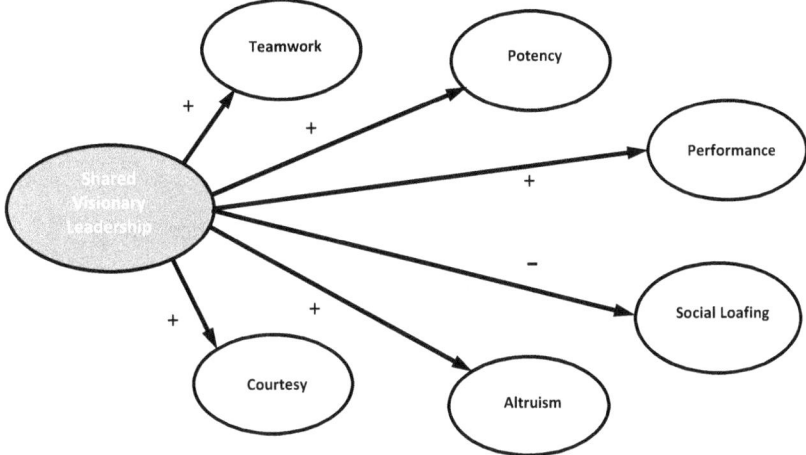

Figure 11 Outcomes of shared visionary leadership in product and process improvement teams

In summarizing the role of moderators, Wang and colleagues (2014), for instance, examine the specific *content* of shared leadership, or in other words, the leadership styles and behaviors that form the foundation of shared leadership. First, they examine what they call traditional shared leadership, which focuses more on transactional exchanges between leaders and followers and encompasses the following leadership styles: initiating structure and consideration, task-oriented leadership behaviors, and contingent reward leadership. The authors find that traditional shared leadership relates to team effectiveness less strongly than new-genre shared leadership (including transformational, visionary, and charismatic leadership behaviors, as well as empowering and authentic leadership) and overall, cumulative shared leadership. Wang and colleagues (2014) also explore the role of a methodological moderator – namely the referent for measuring shared leadership – focusing on (1) teams as the referent, or all members evaluate the team as the entity of influence; (2) each peer as the referent, or each team member rating every other team member on leadership influence; and (3) each member rating him/herself. The authors find no moderating effect for the referent of measurement on the relationship between shared leadership and team effectiveness. Similarly, Wu and colleagues (2020) also examine the moderating role of shared leadership measurement and uncover that the relationship between shared leadership, assessed through an aggregating (or referent shift to the whole team) measurement is weaker ($\rho = .35$) than the relationship between shared leadership assessed with social network analysis and team outcomes ($\rho = .46$).

Overall, when describing the role of shared leadership for overall team effectiveness, the empirical evidence is consistent with the perspective of Pearce and Conger (2003), who argue that shared leadership complements vertical leadership as an essential team characteristic and driver of team effectiveness.

Shared Leadership and Team Performance

Most of the empirical work examining outcomes of shared leadership focuses on team performance, and typically observes a positive relationship between shared leadership and team performance (e.g., Carson et al., 2007; Drescher & Garbers, 2016; Hoch & Kozlowski, 2014; Nicolaides et al., 2014; Pearce & Sims, 2002). Overall, research advocates for, and provides empirical evidence of, a positive and small to moderately strong relationship between shared leadership and various indicators of team performance. For example, researchers report a positive relationship between shared leadership and project completion (Galli et al., 2017), shared leadership and new venture teams' performance (Ensley et al., 2006), shared leadership and virtual R&D teams' performance (Castellano et al., 2021), and shared leadership and subjective assessment of team performance (Carson et al., 2007). As other examples, researchers report a positive relationship between shared leadership and team task performance (Choi et al., 2017), shared leadership and a leader's assessment of team performance (Hoch et al., 2010), as well as shared leadership and teams' financial and strategic performance (Karriker, Madden, & Kattell, 2017).

These findings are also corroborated by meta-analyses (Nicolaides et al., 2014; Wang et al., 2014; D'Innocenzo et al., 2016; Wu et al., 2020), which, over the span of the last ten years, have systematically examined the relationship between shared leadership and various indicators of team effectiveness, with a considerable number of pages dedicated to the relationship between shared leadership and team performance.

The earliest published meta-analysis on shared leadership – that of Wang and colleagues (2014) – aggregates the results from forty studies (with forty-two independent samples). The authors find that shared leadership relates at $r = .16$ and $r = .22$ to team objective and subjective performance, respectively. In a similar manner, in a parallel investigation, Nicolaides and colleagues (2014) meta-analytically aggregate the effect sizes of fifty-four independent samples to estimate an effect size of $r = .28$ for the relationship between shared leadership and overall team performance. In both meta-analyses, the authors also find empirical support for the notion that shared leadership contributes incremental variance to team performance, beyond vertical leadership. In other words, findings indicate that shared leadership positively influences team performance, above and beyond the effect of vertical leadership. The positive relationship between shared leadership and team performance is additionally confirmed by a third meta-analysis, D'Innocenzo and colleagues (2016), who base their examination on forty-three studies and fifty independent effect sizes and report an overall effect size of $r = .21$ for the relationship between shared leadership and overall team performance. In the most recently published meta-analysis, Wu and colleagues (2020) also find a positive relationship between shared leadership and team performance ($r = .30$), basing their examination on twenty-eight independent samples.

Interestingly, however, both Nicolaides and colleagues (2014) and D'Innocenzo and colleagues observe a large variation of the effect sizes in the raw data, with correlations between shared leadership and team performance ranging between −.26 and .75 in Nicolaides et al. (2014) and between −.27 and .60 in D'Innocenzo et al. (2016). Similarly, in primary studies, some authors also fail to find support for a positive relationship between shared leadership and team performance or find evidence for a negative relationship. Fausing and colleagues (2013), for example, find an unexpected non-significant relationship between shared leadership and overall team performance, which probed further reveals a negative relationship between shared leadership and manufacturing team performance, and positive relationship between shared leadership and knowledge team performance. Similarly, Boies, Lvina, and Martens (2010) uncover a non-significant relationship between shared transformational leadership and team performance (but a significant positive relationship with potency), and a negative relationship between shared passive avoidant leadership and team performance, in a business strategy simulation. This raises a number of questions and necessitates the examination of contingencies of the relationship – an issue, which we discuss later in this section.

Shared Leadership and Team Attitudinal Outcomes

Among the many potential team attitudinal outcomes, satisfaction has been of particular interest to scholars. In one of the earlier studies dedicated to shared leadership Avolio, Jung, Murray, and Sivasubramaniam (1996) found that in student project teams, team member satisfaction was positively related to shared leadership. Similarly, Shamir and Lapidot (2003) found that shared leadership was positively related to satisfaction with, as well as trust in, hierarchical leaders, in a study of Israeli military officer training. Serban and Roberts (2016), in a mixed methods study, found shared leadership to be predictive of task satisfaction. Thus, shared leadership has been linked to satisfaction with both team members as well as team leaders. Additionally, scholars have focused on outcomes such as cohesion and trust as examples of team level attitudinal[1] outcomes. Mathieu et al. (2015) found shared leadership to be positively related to team cohesion, in a study of fifty-seven student management teams. In the study described above, Avolio and colleagues (1996) found that teams who displayed more shared leadership also report higher scores on trust and cohesion.

In meta-analytical examinations, the relationship between shared leadership and team attitudinal and behavioral outcomes has also been hypothesized and established. Wang and colleagues (2014) report that shared leadership is "more strongly related to attitudinal outcomes and behavioral processes and emergent states ($\rho = .45$ and $.44$, respectively), compared with subjective and objective (performance) outcomes ($\rho = .25$ and $.18$, respectively)," and go on to conclude that there is a difference in the relationship between shared leadership and team behavioral and attitudinal outcomes, and shared leadership and team performance outcomes. The positive relationship between shared leadership and team behavioral and attitudinal outcomes is also confirmed in another meta-analysis – Wu and colleagues (2020); however, these authors fail to find support for the differential relationship between shared leadership and groups' behavioral and attitudinal outcomes and shared leadership and performance outcomes, concluding that "There are no differences in the strengths of relationships between shared leadership and multiple team outcomes: group behavior processes, attitudinal outcomes, team cognition, and team performance" (p. 58).

Shared Leadership and Team Cognitive Outcomes

Pearce and Ensley (2004) found shared leadership to be positively predictive of potency, in a longitudinal study of innovation teams. Similarly, Lee, Lee, and Seo (2015) report that "knowledge sharing had a partially mediating role between shared leadership and team creativity" (p. 47). Meta-analytic results support the positive relationship between shared leadership and team cognitive outcomes (Wu et al., 2020). The Wu and colleagues study identified nine independent samples, comprising 538 teams, which examined team cognitive outcomes, with a reported relationship of $\rho = .44$. As such, shared leadership appears to be an important predictor of team cognitive outcomes.

---

[1] In the interest of simplicity and presenting a more comprehensive picture, we do not differentiate among attitudinal and affective outcomes, and we also acknowledge that some authors refer to those as emergent team states.

Shared Leadership and Team Behavioral Outcomes

Apart from the umbrella concept of team effectiveness and the more specific focus on team performance, researchers have also examined the relationship between shared leadership and team behavioral outcomes. For example, in a study of seventy-one product and process innovation teams (PPITs), shared visionary leadership was predictive of a number of innovation team behavioral outcomes, including altruistic behavior, coordination-oriented behavior, and other types of positively oriented extra-role behaviors (Pearce & Ensley, 2004). Relatedly, Hooker and Csikszentmihalyi (2003), in a qualitative study of extremely high-performing scientific laboratories, found flow, creativity, and shared leadership to be tightly interconnected. Similarly, Gu et al. (2018) uncovered a positive relationship between shared leadership and team creativity, mediated through knowledge sharing. Finally, Wu and colleagues (2020) identified nine independent samples, comprising 567 teams, which examined team behavioral outcomes, with a reported relationship of $\rho = .28$. Thus, the positive influence of shared leadership on team behavioral outcomes appears to be well supported in extant research.

Moderators of the Shared Leadership – Team Outcomes Relationship

Figure 12 visually summarizes the potential moderators of the shared leadership – team outcomes relationship. To facilitate the review of the state of the literature, we have categorized the moderators into two large groups: substantive moderators, which include team characteristics, team processes, and team (members) attitudes and emergent team states; and methodological moderators, which include team type, shared leadership measure, performance measure, and study setting. In addition, although not traditionally treated as moderators, research discusses differential implications of shared leadership for the different types of team outcomes, which, as noted in Figure 12, can be classified as performance, attitudinal, cognitive, and behavioral outcomes. We start our discussion with the differential implications of shared leadership for different team outcomes, and then we proceed to summarize the role of methodological and team characteristics moderators.

Shared leadership and different team outcomes. Both primary and secondary studies examine the different implications of shared leadership for team performance, team attitudes, team cognition, and team (group) behavioral outcomes. From a theoretical perspective, scholars often argue that shared leadership is differentially related to the various team outcomes criteria. One theoretical reason for this lies in the aforementioned IPO model, which

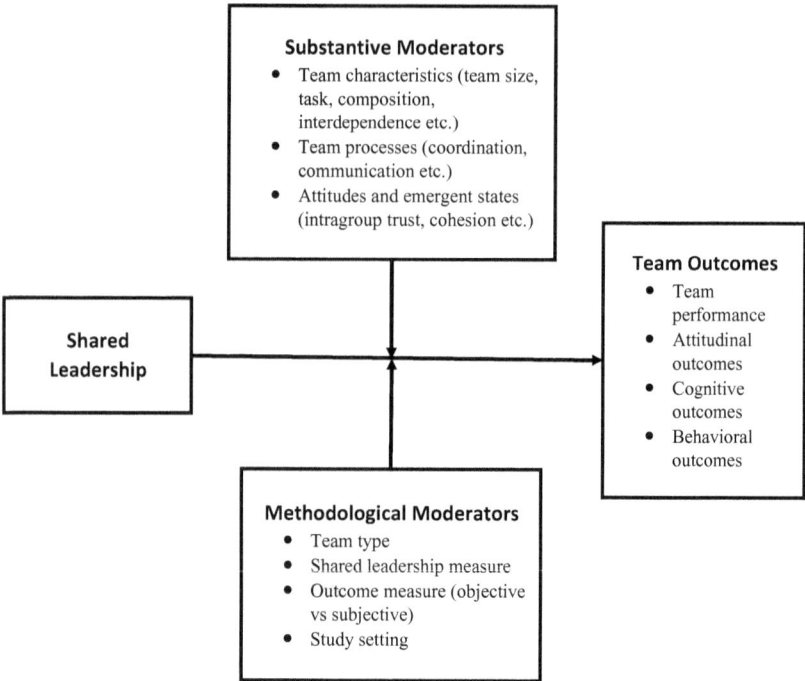

Figure 12 Moderators of the shared leadership – team outcomes relationship

describes team attitudes, cognition, and behaviors as a more proximal, directly influenced by shared leadership, which in turn transfers influence to the more distant outcome of team performance. Other researchers argue that as an emergent team phenomenon, shared leadership is conceptually more similar to teams' attitudes, cognition, and behaviors; hence, it has a stronger relationship with similar concepts. Both arguments have merit, but the empirical evidence is mixed and inconclusive. For example, in their secondary examination, Wang and colleagues (2014) find that shared leadership relates to attitudinal outcomes and behavioral processes and emergent states outcomes stronger (at $r = .39$ and $.37$ respectively) than to objective and subjective team performance (at $r = .22$ and $.16$ respectively). Wang and colleagues also find that the confidence intervals around the reported correlations are not overlapping, thus concluding there is sufficient evidence for differential relationships. On the other hand, in another secondary examination, Wu and colleagues (2020) report that "although shared leadership demonstrates different relationships with group behavior processes ($\rho = .28$), attitudinal outcomes ($\rho = .25$), team cognition ($\rho = .44$), and team performance ($\rho = .37$), their 95% confidence intervals overlap with one another." The same authors go on to conclude that there is no evidence that there is difference in the relationship between shared leadership and the different team outcomes and call for additional research to clarify the extant conflicting results.

Substantive moderators of the shared leadership – team outcomes relationship: team characteristics. Substantive moderators in the relationship between shared leadership and team outcomes can significantly influence how effective shared leadership is within a team. This section highlights some of the findings, although the examples given here should not be treated as an exhaustive list. For example, team characteristics, such as team size, team composition, task interdependence, and task complexity have often been positioned as important factors, which can influence the effectiveness of shared leadership. Larger teams, for example, might face more challenges in coordinating and communicating effectively under shared leadership, while smaller teams might find it easier to share leadership roles, which would suggest that the influence of shared leadership would be stronger in smaller teams. However, as noted by Nicolaides and colleagues, team size "can be both an asset and a liability for teams" (p. 926). Thus, in primary studies Lorinkova and Bartol (2021) find that smaller teams reach and sustain higher levels of shared leadership throughout their life cycle. In their secondary analysis, however, Nicolaides et al. (2014) fail to find evidence for an interaction effect of shared leadership and team size.

Another team factor that can potentially interact with shared leadership and amend its effects on team outcomes is the characteristics of the team task. The argument here is that shared leadership may be more appropriate in some situations, and not in others. Specifically, task complexity may be an important factor, because shared leadership is a complex, team-level phenomenon, more time-consuming in its emergence and development than traditional vertical leadership, likely benefiting teams with more complex tasks, which require higher levels of interactions and coordination among team members. Similar to the moderating role of team size, however, the moderating role of task complexity does not warrant a definitive conclusion. For example, in their secondary examination, based on forty-two independent samples, Wang and colleagues (2014) uncovered a positive relationship between work complexity and the effect size of shared leadership with team effectiveness. On the other hand, in another secondary examination, D'Innocenzo et al. (2016) find a significant *negative* effect of task complexity on the magnitude of the shared leadership – team performance relationship. Examples from primary studies are similarly inconclusive. As a result, researchers agree on the notion that task complexity is an important moderator to consider when studying shared leadership and its influences; however, the specific role of task complexity is still to be found.

Another critical moderator in the relationship between shared leadership and team effectiveness is task interdependence. It refers to the degree to which team members are dependent on one another to complete their work. This concept becomes particularly important in shared leadership models, as it influences how team members interact, collaborate, and share responsibilities. With high task interdependence, the sharing of knowledge and skills becomes vital. Shared leadership fosters an environment where multiple members contribute their expertise, leading to more informed decision-making and problem-solving. In addition, high task interdependence encourages team members to collaborate more closely. In such settings, shared leadership can be more effective because team members are already reliant on each other for information, resources, and support. Meta-analysis, however, do not find a conclusive support for the positive role of task interdependence (e.g., D'Innocenzo et al., 2016).

Team virtuality, referring to the extent to which team members use digital communication technologies to interact and collaborate with each other, often across different locations, is another important moderator of the relationship between shared leadership and team effectiveness. The rise of remote work and global teams has made understanding the impact of team virtuality on shared leadership more crucial. Different theoretical arguments can be put forward on the role of virtuality in teams. On the one hand, communication challenges, due to the lack of face-to-face interaction, can impede the development of trust and mutual understanding in virtual teams. This can affect how shared leadership is established and maintained within the team, suggesting the need for more traditional leadership in highly virtual teams. On the other hand, as suggested by Pearce and Conger (2003), when teams feel empowered to share leadership responsibilities, they communicate more and interact more frequently, which in turn positively influences a number of team outcomes, including members' satisfaction, commitment to the team, and performance. We are not aware of any meta-analysis examining the moderating role of team virtuality; primary investigations, however, report inconclusive results. In an experimental study, Drescher and Garbers (2016) find that shared leadership leads to higher performance and greater satisfaction in virtual teams than in face-to-face teams. In a field study, Hoch and Kozlowski (2014) argue that the positive relationship between shared leadership and team performance increases as virtuality increases, yet fail to find support for this hypothesis.

Team size and team tenure are two team characteristics that have garnered researchers' attention in their quest for explaining team factors. As noted by a host of teams' researchers, team size can be both an asset and a liability (e.g., Maier, 1967; Lorinkova & Bartol, 2021; Shaw, 1981). Larger teams, for example, have larger decision-making and processing capabilities and also include more team members with diverse viewpoints and experience, which can facilitate innovation, flexibility, and creativity. Communication and coordination problems, however, are exacerbated in larger teams, and because individual contributions are less visible in larger teams, members are less likely to contribute individual efforts to the team task (Karau & Williams, 1993; Kidwell & Bennett, 1993). Primary studies generally find that larger teams report lower levels of shared leadership (e.g., Karriker et al., 2017; Lorinkova & Bartol, 2021), whereas meta-analytical examinations find that team size does not appear to augment the effect of shared leadership on team performance (Nicolaides et al., 2014). As far as team tenure is concerned, the same authors find that team tenure reduces the positive effect of shared leadership on team performance, suggesting that the positive effects of shared leadership may be time dependent – an issue we discuss later.

Overall, researchers agree on the notion that team characteristics such as team size, team tenure, task interdependence and complexity, team virtuality, and similar issues may significantly impact the effectiveness of shared leadership. However, definitive empirical evidence regarding the impact of these moderators remains elusive. Additionally, moderators such as team composition, or the diversity of skills, personalities, and backgrounds in a team, may impact how shared leadership translates into team outcomes. Teams with a mix of complementary skills and perspectives may find it easier to establish shared leadership, yet teams with diverse skillsets and personality may need higher levels of shared leadership to guide their interactions. Therefore, understanding the complexity of how shared leadership emerges and operates in teams with different characteristics is an important agenda for future research.

Substantive moderators of the shared leadership – team outcomes relationship: team processes. Team processes are usually discussed as antecedents or outcomes of shared leadership, although examples of team processes as moderators of the effects of shared leadership can also be found. The role of team processes as antecedents is discussed in the previous section of this Element. In that section we also highlight some of the team processes that have been examined as outcomes of shared leadership. As far as moderation is concerned, Hoch, Pearce, and Welzel (2010) found coordination (as well as team age diversity) to moderate the relationship between shared leadership and team effectiveness. Another example for a team process treated as a moderator can be found in the work of Michalache and colleagues (2014), who examined the role of shared leadership in top-management teams (TMTs) as a predictor of organizational ambidexterity (or, the extent to which organizations engage in both exploratory and exploitative innovation). These authors report that the effect of shared leadership on organizational ambidexterity is mediated by conflict management style and decision-making comprehensiveness. Further, they found "the interaction term between TMT shared leadership and connectedness has a positive and significant effect on TMT cooperative management style ($\beta = 0.23$, $p < 0.01$) and ... a positive and significant effect of the interaction between TMT shared leadership and connectedness on TMT decision comprehensiveness ($\beta = 0.23$, $p < 0.01$)" (Michalante et al., 2014, p. 140).

Among the numerous team attitudes, cognition, and emergent states that have been studied, team trust has probably garnered the most attention. Closely related to team trust is the concept of psychological safety, with high trust and safety potentially enhancing collaboration and the willingness to take on leadership roles. The problem with studying trust as a moderator is that unlike team characteristics (team size, tenure, autonomy, interdependence, and similar, to name a few), which are independent from shared leadership, trust, as a relational factor is linked to shared leadership; trust can precede shared leadership, thus serving as an antecedent of shared leadership, but trust can also be the consequence of shared leadership. Trust can also exist independently from shared leadership; for example, if team members know each other and have worked together on previous projects or different teams. Finally, similar to shared leadership, trust can also be treated as an emergent team state, which evolves over time, changing and influencing changes in shared leadership. In fact, in one of the few longitudinal studies, examining shared leadership development, Drescher and colleagues (2014) suggest that positive development in team trust is one of the routes through which changes in shared leadership bring benefits to team performance. In their meta-analytical examination, Wu and colleagues (2020) uncovered that intragroup trust moderates the positive relationship between shared leadership and team outcomes, "such that this relationship is more positive when intragroup trust is higher rather than lower" (p. 58). Regardless of how trust is treated, however, there is conclusive evidence in research that shared leadership and trust in teams are positively related (Drescher et al., 2014; Wu et al., 2020). Similar to trust, team social support – or the extent to which team members care for and encourage each other – has been found to accentuate the emergence and the positive effects of shared leadership (Carson et al., 2007; Lorinkova & Bartol, 2021).

Methodological moderators of the shared leadership – team outcomes relationship. Primary studies seldom examine methodological moderators, and instead usually focus on what are often called substantive moderators or, as we refer to, team characteristics, behaviors, and attitudes. Meta-analysis, however, has placed a lot of attention to methodological moderators, in an attempt to clarify the specifics of the shared leadership–team outcomes relationship. One of the more frequently examined methodological moderators is the specific shared leadership measurement. Wang and colleagues (2014) investigated the moderating role of the shared leadership measurement referent (the whole team as the referent for measuring shared leadership, each peer as the referent, and each member rating him/herself) but did not find any differences, concluding that "the relationship between shared leadership and team effectiveness did not differ across the various referents" (p. 190). Team type has also frequently been examined and found to moderate relationships between antecedents and team outcomes. Wang and colleagues did not explicitly hypothesize but found that there was no significant difference in shared leadership effectiveness in student versus work teams. A similar conclusion was reached by Nicolaides and colleagues, who examined the role of shared leadership in three different types of teams such as decision making, action, and project teams, but found that team type did not interact with shared leadership to predict team performance. In the same study, sample type: field versus school (which coincides with work vs. student teams) also did not have a moderating role on the effect of shared leadership. Sample type, however, was found to exert a significant moderating effect in the study of D'Innocenzo et al. (2016), with shared leadership effect on team performance being higher for field, as compared to classroom/lab samples. In the most-recent meta-analysis, Wu and colleagues (2020) fail to support the moderating role of sample/team type and report that "the relationship between shared leadership and team outcomes does not differ across the different team settings" (p. 59). It appears that in the majority of the published work, shared leadership appears to be equally effective across different types of teams. Similarly, it appears that the measurement of the specific team outcomes – namely objective versus subjective – does not significantly influence the relationship between shared leadership and team outcomes. Although effect size is slightly higher for subjectively assessed team outcomes, the difference between subjective and objective assessment is not significantly different.

The role of time: temporal dynamics of shared leadership. It is important to understand how time affects the patterns and effectiveness of shared leadership in groups, because scholars have highlighted that shared leadership is a time-varying, inherently dynamic team process (Carson et al., 2007; Pearce & Conger, 2003; Pearce, 2004; Pearce et al., 2023; Pearce & van Knippenberg, 2024; Pearce, van Knippenberg, & Kirchoff, 2024). Yet, few studies in extant research focus on the dynamic nature of shared leadership to explain how shared leadership changes over time. A notable exception is the study of Drescher et al. (2014), who found that positive changes in shared leadership were associated with positive changes in group performance, with the relationship partially mediated by positive changes in group trust. In another study (although not longitudinal by design) Wu and Cormican (2021), studying twenty-six engineering project-design teams, found that the stage of the project life cycle influences the positive relationship between shared leadership and team effectiveness, such that this relationship is stronger at the early phase of the project. Additionally, in a study examining sixty-six self-managed executive MBA teams, Wang et al. (2017) found that shared leadership enabled team learning behaviors at the early stages of teams' work together, but not at the middle and later stages of the task. In perhaps the most notable study, which examines shared leadership dynamic effectiveness, Lorinkova and Bartol (2021) study how shared leadership changes over the course of self-managed project teams' life cycle and how the change in shared leadership related to team performance. In particular, they find that shared leadership increases early in the team's life cycle, peaks around the midpoint, and then decreases in the later phase, with this non-uniform, approximating inverted U-shape change pattern positively relating to team performance. Although the four studies explained previously in the section reach somewhat differing conclusions, one common theme runs across the studies: shared leadership is an important predictor of team effectiveness; however, additional research is needed to uncover the specific role of time.

Shared Leadership and Individual Outcomes

The majority of shared leadership research focuses on group/team-level outcomes, which is consistent with the nature of shared leadership. However, shared leadership also has significant implications for individuals. One of the most widely researched individual-level variables in organizational behavior is individual satisfaction; to date, several studies have examined the effects of shared leadership on satisfaction. For example, Shamir and Lapidot (2003), sampling participants in an Israeli military officer training, found that shared leadership was positively related to satisfaction with, as well as trust in, hierarchical leaders. Individual learning and creativity have also been examined as outcomes of shared leadership at the individual level. Thus, Peter, Braun, and Frey (2015) and Gu et al. (2018) found shared leadership to be positively related to individual creativity, whereas Liu, Hu, Li, Wang, and Lin (2014) found that shared leadership related positively to individual (and team) learning. Another outcome that has garnered researchers' attention is knowledge sharing: Coun, Peters, and Blomme (2019) report a direct relationship between shared leadership and individual perceptions of knowledge sharing in teams.

Individual self-efficacy and skill development have also been linked to shared leadership. For example, George et al. (2002) found shared leadership to be directly related to follower self-efficacy, whereas Klein, Zeigert, Knight, and Xiao (2006) found shared leadership to be positively associated with the skill development of junior medical staff, which was also found in Pearce et al.

(2014). Finally, Hooker and Csikszentmihalyi (2003), in a study of R&D laboratories, found mimetic effects of shared leadership: that is, in their own laboratories, followers "mimicked" the encouragement of shared leadership learned from the lead scientist in their original PhD training laboratory. Accordingly, shared leadership has been highlighted as the enabler of multiple positive individual-level outcomes.

Shared Leadership and Organizational Outcomes

Studies that discuss the relationship between shared leadership and organizational-level outcomes mainly focus on shared leadership in TMTs and entrepreneurial teams. In their examination of new venture teams, Hmieleski et al. (2012), for example, link shared authentic leadership in top management teams to positive team affective tone, which in turn translated into the better performance of new ventures. In an earlier, two-sample study, which examined 66 and 154 startups' top management teams respectively, Ensley and colleagues (2006) uncovered that different types of shared leadership (directive, transactive, transformational and empowering) were positively related to new venture performance. The study of Mihalache and colleagues (2014) can be described as another example of how shared leadership of the TMTs positively influences outcomes at the organizational level, namely organizational ambidexterity. Several qualitative studies have also examined organizational outcomes of shared leadership. For example, Pearce et al. (2019) found the paradoxical combination of vertical and shared leadership to be important to organizational success. Similarly, Pearce (2014) identified shared leadership as an important ingredient in the success of Southwest Airlines. Relatedly, Bligh and Pearce (2014) found the shared leadership culture developed at Panda Restaurant Group to be a critical component in the success of the organization. In conclusion, at the organizational level, shared leadership, especially in top management teams, has been highlighted as enabler of organizational performance.

Summary of the Empirical Examination of Outcomes of Shared Leadership

Significant strides have been made regarding the empirical examination of the outcomes of shared leadership. Naturally, many of these studies have focused on group/team-level outcomes, but some have also investigated individual-level outcomes and organization-level outcomes. In general, shared leadership appears to have positive effects on a wide variety of outcomes. Moreover, the effects of shared leadership appear to be stronger than the effects of vertical leadership (e.g., Pearce & Sims, 2002). Interestingly, several moderators of the shared leadership to outcomes relationship have been posited and investigated, yielding greater insight into the shared leadership-outcomes relationships.

In total, shared leadership shows considerable promise for enhancing organizational outcomes, be they at the individual-, team- or organizational-level of analysis. In the next section, we highlight what we consider to be the most important future steps regarding the investigation of shared leadership.

5 Shared Leadership: A Future Research Agenda

There have been sufficient quantitative studies of shared to result in the publication of four meta-analyses (D'Innocenzo, Mathieu, & Kukenberger, 2014; Nicolaides et al., 2014; Wang, Waldman & Zhang, 2014; Wu, Cormican, & Chen, 2020). There have also been many qualitative studies of shared leadership published in the literature. For example, Pearce, Manz, and Sims (2014) published ten comprehensive qualitative studies of shared leadership, as well as eleven more concise studies. Nonetheless, the field is at an important point to take stock of the state of where we are and, more importantly, where we should be heading. While much has been done, the future research agenda is replete with opportunities. In this section, we identify what we consider to be the most critical issues for moving the field forward.

First, however, it is useful to grade the current state of the science on shared leadership relative to the research agenda specified by Conger and Pearce (2003) in the final chapter of their book, *Shared Leadership: Reframing the Hows and Whys of Leadership*. In this chapter, Conger and Pearce identified seven research domains for the study of shared leadership, including the articulation of scores of more specific research questions. Table 3 provides a comprehensive summary of the domains and questions Conger and Pearce generated to jumpstart the inquiry into shared leadership. While there have been significant advances, we would characterize the progress made to date as modest (see Table 3). The upshot is that most of the research questions posed by Conger and Pearce have barely been addressed, which leaves a fertile field for future studies.

Overarching Critical Issues for Future Studies of Shared Leadership

There are seven critical issues regarding the future study of shared leadership: (1) definition drift, (2) weak qualitative studies, (3) need for greater understanding of antecedents, (4) over-focus on direct effects, (5) lack of multi-level studies, (6) lack of studies of the dark side of shared leadership, and (7) lack of truly longitudinal studies. We discuss each of these seven issues in the following paragraphs.

Table 3 The shared leadership research agenda scorecard and key questions for moving the field forward

Research Domain	Key Questions	Status of the Field
Relationship between shared and vertical leadership	• Does vertical leadership catalyze shared leadership? • Does lack of catalyzation from above preclude shared leadership? • Is it possible to witness shared leadership in the absence of vertical leadership? • Is vertical leadership a barrier to shared leadership? • What roles should a vertical leader display to encourage shared leadership? • Can vertical and shared leadership complement each other?	Minimal work has been done to date. Qualitative studies point to an important relationship but the methods are loose. Quantitative studies clearly document a relationship but many questions remain. **Grade: C**
Dynamics of shared leadership	• What are the bases of shared leadership? • What are the roles of shared leadership? • What are the influence tactics of shared leadership? • What triggers leadership transitions for shared leadership? • Are certain triggers more potent than others? • Do situational characteristics interact with triggers? • What factors facilitate shared leadership?	Very rudimentary work has been done in this area – mainly in area of antecedents. This area needs significant attention. **Grade: D+**

Table 3 (cont.)

Research Domain	Key Questions	Status of the Field
	• What role does task competence play in shared leadership?	
	• What role does task complexity play in shared leadership?	
	• What role does shared knowledge play in shared leadership?	
	• What role do shared mental models play in shared leadership?	
	• What role does transactive memory play in shared leadership?	
	• How do leadership prototypes impact shared leadership?	
	• How are status differentials perceived and treated?	
	• Do personal attraction and familiarity play a role in shared leadership?	
	• How do different types of diversity affect shared leadership?	
	• How does group size impact shared leadership?	
	• Does shared leadership have a life cycle?	

Developing and implementing shared leadership	- What role does culture play in implementing shared leadership? - How is shared leadership different at the small group versus large group or organization level of analysis? - How does organization design affect shared leadership development? - What role do politics play in shared leadership? - Can organizational mavericks or remote locations overcome inertia impeding shared leadership? - What type of performance measurements and rewards promote shared leadership? - How do selection systems affect shared leadership? - What specific actions can vertical leadership take to promote shared leadership? - What specific actions can individuals not in a formal leadership role take to promote shared leadership?	Several factors have been found to contribute to the development of shared leadership but the work is basic and lacks nuance. Primarily studies have simply documented that there are variables related to shared leadership. **Grade: C**
Cross-cultural issues and shared leadership	- How do cultural values affect shared leadership? - What effect do culturally diverse group have on shared leadership? - What effect do regulatory environments have on shared leadership? - What effect do financial markets have on shared leadership? - Are there other factors that vary by culture that impact shared leadership?	Several studies have been conducted outside of North America, documenting that shared leadership exists, as such, in Asia, Africa, Europe and the Middle East. One study examines shared leadership across multiple cultural contexts. This area requires significant future attention. **Grade: C**

Table 3 (cont.)

Research Domain	Key Questions	Status of the Field
Outcomes of shared leadership	• How does shared leadership affect various behaviors? • How does shared leadership impact attitudes? • How does shared leadership affect cognition? • How does shared leadership affect effectiveness? • Are there different effects of shared leadership at different levels of analysis?	This is, not surprisingly, where the most progress has been made to data. Multiple meta-analyses confirm a robust relationship between shared leadership and positive outcomes. **Grade: B−**
Measuring shared leadership	• What are the possibilities for measuring shared leadership? • How do alternative measurement methods compare? • Can simple methodologies capture the essence of shared leadership? • Are different types of measures of shared leadership differentially effective in predicting different types of outcomes? • How can qualitative approaches to measuring shared leadership be enhanced?	Studies have examined alternative ways of measuring shared leadership, yet direct comparisons of alternate protocols are still needed and much is yet to be done. **Grade: C+**
Limits and liabilities of shared leadership	• What are the limits of shared leadership? • What are the liabilities of shared leadership?	Very little has been done in this respect. The initial hesitancy of the field regarding the

- How do knowledge, skills and abilities limit shared leadership?
- How do leadership competencies limit shared leadership?
- How do followership competencies limit shared leadership?
- How does lack of goal alignment within a group limit shared leadership?
- How does lack of goal alignment between a group and a larger organizational group limit shared leadership?
- How does time pressure limit shared leadership?
- How does lack of receptivity to shared leadership limit shared leadership?
- Is shared leadership related to negative outcomes?

concept has been overcome, thus enabling the positive study of shared leadership but the limits and liabilities have a dearth of exploration.

Grade: D–

Definition Drift

There seems to be an addiction to creating definitions and developing new terminology. The shared leadership space is no exception. There is marginal conceptual difference between alternative terms and shared leadership and, overall, the theory of shared leadership has suffered from various definitions which obscure theoretical parsimony, thus also complicating the research agenda.

Several ancillary concepts related to shared leadership have appeared in the literature. These range from collaborative leadership (e.g., Raelin, 2006), to collective leadership (e.g., Contractor et al., 2012), to distributed leadership (e.g., Mehra et al., 2006). Studies, under the auspices of these related terms, however, have documented findings quite similar to those using the shared leadership umbrella term. Pearce and colleagues (2014) attempted to provide an organizing framework for rationalizing such terms: rotated shared leadership, integrated shared leadership, distributed shared leadership, and comprehensive shared leadership (see Figure 3). The field would do well, at this juncture, to focus on the umbrella term of shared leadership, as well as the definition provided by Pearce and Conger (2003, p. 1): "a dynamic, interactive influence process among individuals in groups for which the objective is to lead one another to the achievement of group or organizational goals or both."

Weak Qualitative Studies

Despite the potential for qualitative studies to provide unique insight into phenomena, the vast majority of qualitative studies looking into shared leadership and related concepts are somewhat disappointing in this regard. For example, Pearce et al. (2014) published twenty-one studies of shared leadership in various organizations. Most of the studies can be best described as light (Strauss & Corbin, 1998). They were mainly written for practitioner audiences, so this is no personal attack on the authors of such studies, as their intended purpose seems to have been met, namely, informing practitioners about the usefulness of shifting away from a top-heavy model of leadership. Nonetheless, if we are to move theory forward some well-grounded qualitative studies would be helpful. An exemplar, in this regard, is the Pearce et al. (2019) article.

Need for Greater Understanding of Antecedents

Most of the studies of shared leadership have focused on the outcomes of shared leadership. While investigating outcomes of shared leadership is important, now, there is a more pressing need for future research is regarding the antecedents. While there are a number of theoretical articles that address the antecedents of shared leadership, the empirical work in this area is lagging. Rectifying this is important both scientifically and for practical reasons. To put it more bluntly, the more clearly we understand the antecedents of shared leadership, the more able we are to aid organizational development efforts for shared leadership. Some opportunities in this space are studies that explore different types of leader support, both in the team but also outside of the team, the role of training programs in shared leadership development (these studies would particularly be useful in a longitudinal research design), job design, as well as additional work on ethics and corporate social responsibility as catalysts for shared leadership development.

Over-focus on Direct Effects

Most studies of shared leadership are fairly simple, just investigating one, or a few direct effects, such as the shared leadership-effectiveness relationship (e.g., Ensley, Hmieleski & Pearce, 2006). These were very important early on, but it is now time to move well beyond such studies. The next wave of research on shared leadership needs to have much greater emphasis on both mediators and moderators. This will enable a more fine-grained and comprehensive understanding of what makes shared leadership tick.

Lack of Multi-level Studies

Early in the development of shared leadership theory Pearce (1997) and Pearce and Sims (2000) specifically articulated the multi-level nature of the concept. Even so, the multi-level study of shared leadership has generally been limited to the examination of vertical and shared leadership in tandem (e.g., Ensley et al., 2006; Pearce & Sims, 2002). While such studies are useful, they lack the nuance of the real-life enactment of shared leadership. For example, Bligh, Pearce, and Kohles (2006) theorized that the specific individual-level phenomenon in groups/teams would morph through meso-processes into the display of shared leadership, yet no known studies have fully investigated this angle (see Figure 13). The point here is that there is far more to be learned from investigating the multi-level nature of shared leadership and that the extant literature is lacking in this regard.

Lack of Studies of the Dark Side of Shared Leadership

Pearce and Conger (2003) speculated that there would almost certainly be limits and liabilities associated with shared leadership, yet this is an area that has received scant attention. This is not surprising, but it is an open area for future studies. As just one example, it would be useful to examine abusive types of

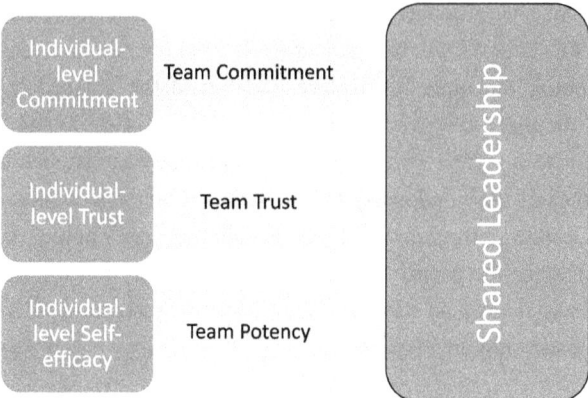

Figure 13 Example multi-level psychological processes and shared leadership

leadership enacted through shared leadership processes and illuminate their effects on such things as individual and team outcomes. We expect that the results would be similar, but perhaps more profound, than those identified in the vertical leadership literature. Further, drawing on the notion of the shared leadership paradox outlined in the Pearce et al. (2019) article, there are likely to be other potential paradoxes that would be interesting to investigate.

Lack of Truly Longitudinal Studies

Shared leadership is a dynamic process, and the only way to truly understand dynamic processes is through longitudinal examination (Pearce & van Knippenberg, 2024; Pearce, van Knippenberg, & van Ginkel, 2023; Pearce, van Knippenberg, & Kirchoff, 2024). While most quantitative studies of shared leadership have employed quasi-longitudinal designs – they collect independent and dependent variables at slightly different times – these designs are primarily concerned with mitigating concerns about common method variance. Truly longitudinal designs, where the same variables are collected repeatedly over an extended time period, are what we need next, in order to gain insight into the dynamic process of shared leadership (see Pearce et al., 2023 for a comprehensive discussion of this issue).

Research Imperatives for Shared Leadership

While previous studies of shared leadership have certainly moved the scientific dialogue forward, future studies need to go much further. In general, the field has done a respectable job of establishing that shared leadership is a valid construct and that it has predictive validity, above and beyond leadership from a vertical leader. It is indeed time for a reboot that will clarify, codify, and elevate the rigor of studies on shared leadership theory. Here, however, we offer four important imperatives and one alternative perspective regarding shared leadership theory and research.

Research Imperatives

First, the measurement of shared leadership requires serious attention. Pearce and Conger laid out a menu of options for the measurement of shared leadership, yet most studies have focused on relatively simple measures that are then assessed using fairly simple analytic processes. In many ways, the research design often appears to be aimed at expediency, rather than thoughtfully considering the research design to truly gather information in such a way that measures the propositions or questions that will move the field forward. While meta-analyses have compared measurement issues, directly comparing and contrasting multiple methods is essential as we move forward.

Second, perhaps what has limited the research to date is the dearth of high-quality qualitative studies, to enable a more robust understanding of the fine-grained mechanisms for refined study with more precise quantitative methods. Nonetheless, significant theory does provide guidance in this respect, even without grounded research to aid it.

Third, shared leadership is a multi-level phenomenon, yet few studies have treated it as such. This is a gaping hole in the entire ken. While studies have acknowledged the multi-level nature of shared leadership, the empirical examination of shared leadership as a multi-level phenomenon leaves much room for improvement. For instance, multi-level phenomenon, by their very nature, requires time to develop; yet time has not been much of a consideration (see Pearce et al., 2023), which brings us to our fourth point.

Fourth, future research must focus far more on truly longitudinal designs. By this, we do not mean designs that merely capture independent and dependent variables at different points in time. Rather, we mean collecting repeated measures of shared leadership to more fully understand it as an unfolding social process, as recommended by Pearce et al. (2023). This is an essential issue for future studies.

Finally, future studies of shared leadership need to be far more comprehensive. The vast majority of the extant literature is rather simple, yet social dynamics are inherently complex. If we desire to truly move theory forward, we need to incorporate more holistic approaches to our research studies. Conger and Pearce (2003), for instance, outlined seven major considerations for the examination of shared leadership, with scores of research questions regarding the study of shared leadership. Current research has nibbled at this research agenda. Future research would do well to tackle these issues in a more comprehensive manner. For example, more research examining antecedents, outcomes, moderators, and mediators simultaneously would enable a much more textured understanding of shared leadership in action.

A New Frontier for Shared Leadership

We need to complete the paradigm shift that is underway in the field of leadership: all leadership is shared leadership; it is simply a matter of degree. While much has been learned through examining vertical leaders, it is clear from the evidence that not investigating shared leadership processes as part of the social leadership equation is missing a very important aspect of social leadership. For example, Pearce and Sims (2002) directly compared the amount of variance of team effectiveness explained by vertical versus shared leadership and revealed that shared leadership is a more robust predictor. Multiple meta-analysis studies reinforce this finding (e.g., Nicolaides et al., 2014; Wang et al., 2014).

There are three fundamental dimensions along which the sharing of leadership can be assessed. First, is the *centralization of power*. With entirely centralized power, for instance, the amount of shared leadership approaches zero. Logically, it follows that in an environment where power is entirely decentralized, shared leadership is far more likely to develop. The second dimension, *level of engagement*, describes how actively team members are involved in leading one another. At one extreme would be un-engagement, or apathy, while on the other end would be full engagement, and a concomitant high level of shared leadership. The third dimension is *type of influence*, and it ranges from rudimentary influence, which is typically focused on base influence strategies such as being directive, to comprehensive influence strategies relying on a full range of situationally appropriate influence, including such influence strategies as vision, inspiration, empowerment, and transactional engagement (see Figure 5).

The more comprehensive the influence type, the more potential there is for shared leadership. Taken together, high centralization of power, low engagement, and rudimentary types of influence would be characteristic of low levels of shared leadership, while low power centralization, high levels of engagement, and comprehensive types of influence are characteristic of high levels of shared leadership. Figure 14 provides a three-dimensional view of the fundamental components that comprise the continuum of shared leadership.

By framing all leadership as shared leadership, using these three dimensions as a foil, we anticipate far greater understanding of social leadership processes and effects. This type of framing is poised to provide the next giant leap in the scientific study of leadership.

Shared Leadership 2.0

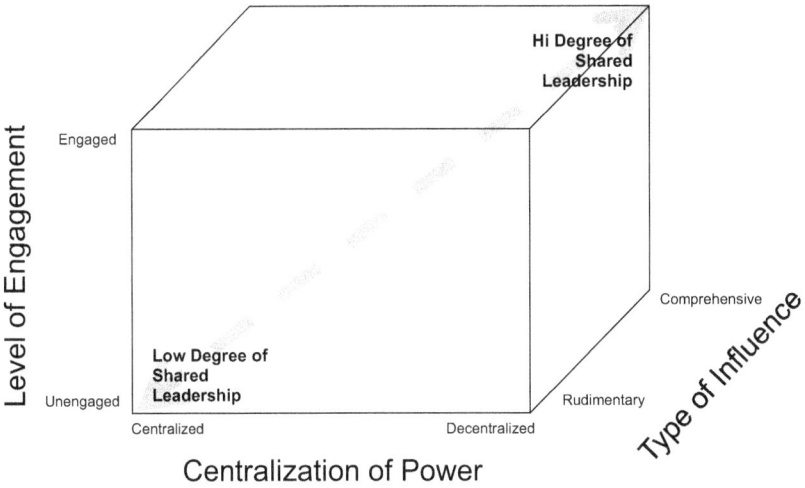

Figure 14 All leadership is shared ... it's just a matter of degree

Summary Regarding Future Research on Shared Leadership

The most insightful issue for the future research on leadership is framing of all social leadership is shared leadership, that it is just a matter of degree. Of course, it is perfectly valid to focus future research on *just* vertical leaders, but such research needs to acknowledge the incomplete nature of the data, as vertical leaders are clearly part of the equation of shared leadership. More robust qualitative studies that can enrich the foundations of research in this area are very much needed. Building on such discoveries, quantitative studies need to attend to far more complex and nuanced examinations of the phenomenon. No matter what, we encourage scholars to examine the table detailing the research domains and research questions for shared leadership provided in this section as a source of inspiration for future research studies.

6 Putting Shared Leadership into Practice

Although a large part of this Element is devoted to the science of shared leadership, we are practitioners at heart and are strong proponents of evidence-based management, as well as evidence-based leadership. After all, is it not the point to move the findings of research into practice? As such, in this section, we shift to providing practical advice gleaned from the findings presented in Sections 3 and 4, designed to help people understand how to evaluate their current state, design and implement potential solutions, and thus reap the benefits of shared leadership in organizations.

We encourage those who are interested in increasing shared leadership in their own organizations to view it as occurring along a series of continuums, where one side of the continuum is *no shared leadership*, and the other end is *all shared leadership*. Then, you can evaluate where you fall on that continuum, and using the antecedents that are already provided in Section 3, or even try out some of the additional suggestions for research that we offer in Section 5, you can decide how to alter various factors that support shared leadership and measure the outcomes of the changes. It is important to keep in mind that shared leadership is a multi-factor/multi-level organizational experience, and that merely saying that "we share leadership" or that "I share leadership" is not usually enough to ensure a lasting experience of shared leadership. As such, we will use this section to offer some more tactical advice. Keep in mind that this is not exhaustive, but it will definitely offer a starting point, and a mindset, that will help to develop the possibility of shared leadership in almost any organization.

We organize this advice according to four major categories: (1) individual-level advice, (2) group/team-level advice, (3) organization-level advice, and (4) human resources practice advice (see Figure 15). Using these four overarching categories, in Figure 15 we provide a brief guide to action for the development of shared leadership in organizations.

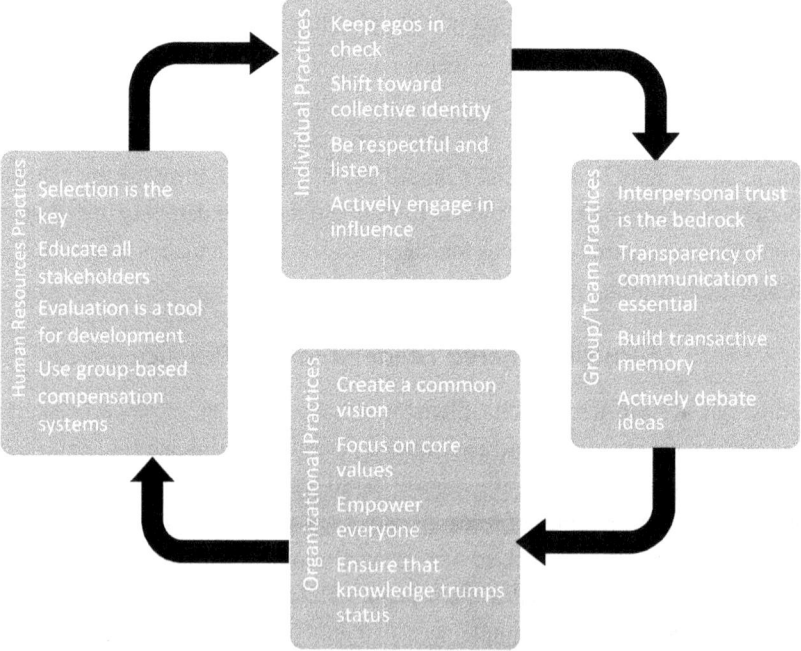

Figure 15 Summary of practices to support shared leadership
Adapted from: Pearce, Manz & Sims (2014). *Share, Don't Take the Lead*

Individual-Level Advice

Every social process begins with individuals. If individuals refuse to participate with others in social processes, such as shared leadership, the process will be rocky, at best. In this regard, individual egos, while essential, must be kept in check for shared leadership to thrive. This is easy to say but much harder to put into practice, especially over the medium- to long-term. For example, smart people, with a high need for achievement, that is, those that are essential to enabling progress, often find it challenging to keep their egos in check in team-based work. Nevertheless, setting individual egos aside, at least temporarily, is essential for moving from the "I" to the "we" as a reference point for shared leadership; That is, there needs to be a shift toward collective identity. In today's knowledge intensive work environment, the vast majority of work product relies upon collaborative efforts between capable and motivated individuals (see Pearce, 2004, 2010), and this requires moving beyond the egos of individuals.

Beyond individual ego suspension and collective identification, individuals involved in shared leadership must have well-honed listening skills and they must be open to others' ideas, thoughts, opinions, and perspectives (while ultimately also being able to evaluate such ideas objectively in order to bring focus to the team efforts). Finally, it is imperative that anyone involved shared leadership must be a capable leader in their own right. In other words, everybody involved in the shared leadership process must be able to effectively engage in appropriately influencing other members of the team. For shared leadership to be optimally effective, depending on the knowledge, skills, and abilities on the individuals involved and the task requirements of the situation at hand, everybody needs to be an active and engaged leader. While it is clearly possible to dig deeper, these are the core pieces of advice for individuals, for the practice of shared leadership.

Group/Team-Level Advice

At the team-level of analysis trust is the key issue. Trust is essential for shared leadership. If individuals do not trust one another, shared leadership is, at best, a non-starter. The reality, however, is probably much worse. When individuals in teams do not trust one another, they tend to undermine each other and derail potential progress. In fact, trust is such a foundational force in social interactions that it has even been linked to the economic development of nations, such that nations with low trust levels have extremely poor economic outcomes. As groups and teams are the building blocks of larger social entities, such as departments and organizations, they are the key units in which trust must be built. Here, transparency of communication, where there is a norm of being respectful and listening, is fundamental to creating a trusting environment. This facilitates knowledge sharing and simultaneously discourages second-guessing, each of which are essential to creating a trusting environment.

Beyond a trusting and open environment, for shared leadership to be especially effective, it requires what scholars call transactive memory. Transactive memory entails being aware of which team members have which knowledge, skills, and abilities that are relevant to the tasks of the team. Transactive memory is critical to ensure smooth leadership transitions between the most appropriate team members, and it also helps to prevent power hording by a particular individual or subset of the team.

Early in team life, it is not always reasonable to expect well-developed transactive memory within the team. In this case, we advocate encouraging the active debate and discussion of ideas, thoughts, and perspectives and actively encouraging team norms that stress the importance of constructively challenging of each other's input. We also advocate the creation of opportunities for team members to get to know each other in a structured setting outside of the boundaries of the main focus of work. These are the key pieces of group/team-level advice we advocate regarding shared leadership.

Organization-Level Advice

Shifting our attention to larger collectives of people, like organizations, brings different issues to the fore, with respect to shared leadership deployment. Here the paramount issue is ensuring that there is a clear, compelling, and commonly understood vision regarding the driving purpose of the organization. Without a clear and shared vision, groups/teams at any level of the organization will undoubtedly work at cross-purposes (or worse). With all of that said, shared leadership can be harnessed to facilitate the creation of a common or shared vision, thereby ensuring the vision is compelling, is complete, and enjoys true buy-in from core constituencies, as elaborated by Berson, Waldman and Pearce (2016).

Beyond shared vision, shared values are also critically important in organization-wide shared leadership practice. Shared values are one of the very few true long-term sources of competitive advantage for organizations. Each organization should focus on crafting values that are unique to their overarching purpose and that facilitate alignment of shared leadership throughout the organization. The only specific values we recommend in this regard are a focus on fairness and ethics – these were found to be useful antecedents to shared leadership as shown in Section 3. Other than these basic values each organization will need to carefully consider which values should be emphasized and encouraged. For instance, for some it will be a focus on creativity, while for others it might entail a focus on reliability. The upshot is that shared cultural values provide an organizing mechanism though which shared leadership can be developed and leveraged to enhance competitive advantage.

Empowerment is another key consideration from the organizational-level point of view. We advocate empowering nearly everyone in organizations, at least somewhat. It is indeed an unusual person (not to say that they don't exist) that is not capable of taking on some leadership responsibility and thereby positively contributing to organizational success, and most people will clearly say that they value *being* empowered over almost any other organizational experience. This is why we believe that knowledge, skills, and abilities should almost always trump organizational status. This, of course, can be uncomfortable for novice organizational leaders but it can also be rather rewarding, in that through the process of empowering they gain loyalty from their followers, the possibility of new ways of solving old problems, buy-in to shared goals, and many other positive outcomes that are too extensive to list here. In summary, these are the key pieces of advice we advocate for shared leadership deployment, from the organizational-level point of view.

Human Resources Practice Advice

Human resource policies and practices are an area that requires special attention when it comes to shared leadership. Most human resource professionals, for instance, are overly focused on creating stifling bureaucratic fiefdoms that only serve to enhance the power of the human resource function. These proclivities must be weeded out if shared leadership is to thrive. Thus, selection is the single most important thing that can be done, from an HR perspective, when it comes to shared leadership, and a very useful place to start is on selecting the right HR professionals – people who understand not just the legal components of HR but also keep up on the organizational development innovations in their field, understand assessment processes, and clearly comprehend that they are in a support role.

Different circumstances (different visions and different core values), quite naturally, require different types of individuals. As such, person/job fit, person/organization fit, and person/situation fit are the key concerns when it comes to selection. Unfortunately, most people are abysmal at selecting the right people. In this the fault lies both with HR but also with the various functions working with HR to select people. We know that people are subconsciously biased towards people who resemble them, who have similar educational backgrounds, who have had parallel organizational paths, and so on. But that native human nature is not going to always result in the best hire for both the job, but also to support a shared leadership environment. Therefore, organizational leaders need to work hand in hand with HR to find the people who truly embody both the values they espouse, who are the people they *need*, not just the ones they *want*.

There are, however, a couple of exemplary organizations – Southwest Airlines and W. L. Gore – that provide strong guidance on how to get it right. Pearce et al. (2014) provide detailed accounts of how these organizations consistently outperform others when it comes to selection and we encourage using them as role models. Beyond selection, shared leadership also benefits greatly from ongoing support in the form of education, training, and development. Most such efforts in organizations focus on appointed leaders or upon people identified as "high potentials" but this is simply insufficient, when it comes to shared leadership. We advocate much more inclusive education, training, and development efforts. Relatedly, evaluation and assessment efforts, which are generally used to justify remuneration for people, need to be broadened to be used much more for developmental purposes. Finally, compensation, in most organizations, needs to be totally rethought. While nearly every organization claims that they value teamwork, precious few actually practice what they preach, and reward people based on team or group outcomes, yet we know that shared vision, goals, and rewards lead to more shared leadership (see Section 3). There are several different ways to build group-based and team-based compensation into organizational HR routines. For example, gainsharing (e.g., O'Bannon & Pearce, 1999) is one such method but each organization will require a tailored approach. Taken together, these are a few of the key human resources practices we advocate for shared leadership success.

Putting It All Together

It is all well and good to think about the science of shared leadership but, ultimately, the most critical issue is putting shared leadership into practice (Pearce & Manz, 2014). Here we have illuminated the key pieces of advice, gleaned from the literature, as well as from our own executive and consulting experience, to help develop, deploy, and embed shared leadership in organizations. We focused this advice on four key areas: individual-level advice, group/team-level advice, organization-level advice, and human resources practice advice. While we broke down these pieces of advice into definable chucks, we believe they work best in concert. With that said, every situation is different and you will need to create your own tailored approach.

7 The Future of Shared Leadership

It was only a few decades ago that shared leadership was considered an anathema by most leadership scholars. There was no interest from the "A" journals in any of the nascent work that had been done, but now, numerous articles on shared leadership (e.g., conceptual, empirical, etc.) can be easily found in all of them. Kuhn (1962) was prescient, in this regard, highlighting both the usefulness and the liabilities of scientific paradigms. Scientific paradigms streamline the process for progress, especially when the progress lies within their boundaries, but are also quite resistant to change, eschewing ideas that do not fall neatly into the paradigm. Nonetheless, academics have now caught up with the reality of shared leadership and it is one of the fastest growing areas of research in the leadership space (see Figure 2). Practitioners, on the other hand, embraced the idea far before the academy did – practitioners are always searching for ways to improve organizations; they are much more pragmatic.

In this Element, we proffered that all leadership is shared leadership; it is just a matter of degree. We highlight the idea that shared leadership occurs on a continuum; using this notion can inform both the research community as well as practitioners on the further investigation and implementation of shared leadership. Looking forward, the question is how quickly they will embrace the next stage of shared leadership research – its conceptualization as a meta-theory. We expect similar reactions to this statement, from both the academic and practitioner communities, respectively, regarding this paradigm shift.

Even though we claim that all leadership is shared leadership, we also believe that there is always a role for leadership from above in an organizational setting, but that this is simply a component of the shared leadership process. We have always been clear that leadership from above is critical to shared leadership (see Pearce, 2004 for a lengthy discussion on the combination of vertical, top-down leadership into the shared leadership process; as well as Pearce, van Knippenberg, & van Ginkel, 2023, for a more recent articulation of this issue).

As we forge further into the age of knowledge work (Drucker, 1969), our models of leadership will continue to evolve to embrace the paradigmatic shift away from the historic perspective which essentially regarded leadership as a top-down role, into leadership as an unfolding social process, that is, the shared leadership perspective. This evolutionary process, as with many others, brings to light several questions beginning with the most simple: Can leadership be shared effectively? The answer to this basic question, clearly, is yes. In fact, the scientific evidence is rather compelling on this question. We provide quite a bit of detail on this issue in Sections 3 and 4 of this Element.

Most of this evidence is quantitative in nature. With that said, one of the more interesting publications on shared leadership in the last decade is the book by Pearce, Manz, and Sims (2014), where they provided qualitative studies of twenty-one organizations, using the shared leadership frame. While we would characterize most these qualitative studies as being on the light-side, from a rigorous scientific point of view, they are nonetheless interesting, and provide clear snapshots of these organizations regarding cultural, business model, leadership values, as well as outcomes, associated with the experience of shared leadership. The scope and variety of organizations represented, from multiple nations, from multiple industries, and from business, not-for profit and governmental sectors, offer us a practical lens by which to evaluate our own organizations as well. Examples include how sharing leadership in Alcoholics Anonymous empowers people to address their addictions more effectively; how medical teams at the University of Maryland shock trauma center handle patients more quickly and safely; how Southwest Airlines corporate culture enables leadership to originate from any level; and how shared leadership plays out in such places as the Republic of South Korea, Switzerland, the Netherlands, and in Afghanistan.

Is developing shared leadership challenging? Yes, it can be. Having said that, we firmly believe that most people are capable of being leaders and that shared leadership is an organizational imperative for the era of knowledge work (Pearce, 2010). Although there will always be circumstances where shared leadership approaches might not work, the research evidence demonstrates that shared leadership, generally, has a positive effect on individual-, group/team-, and organizational-level outcomes, including organizational performance. That positive benefit will be more and more important as organizations become increasingly interconnected, people dive deeper into technological solutions to traditional work, yet where they still want to feel that they are part of something significant (Pearce & van Knippenberg, 2023). We can look back to how societies changed with the Industrial Revolution and see similar shifts today – people are no different in their needs from then to now – and shared leadership is a way to provide the connection to people and their work that transcends the passing of time and technology.

Does this mean that shared leadership is a panacea? No. There is no such thing as a panacea for all organizational woes. Are there circumstances where we do not advocate shared leadership? Yes. For example, there are certainly individual contributor roles that do not require shared leadership. In fact, force fitting shared leadership over any particular potential organizational process simply does not seem wise. Nonetheless, we might imagine that even for individual contributor roles there may be occasions when such individual contributors might be brought together in a task force to identify ways to improve – and this situation would most likely benefit from shared leadership. As such, shared leadership seems like it would have, at a minimum, some type of role in most peoples' organizational lives.

We further believe that certain other preconditions are fruitful for shared leadership to flourish. For instance, it seems important that the individuals involved should have well-developed knowledge, skills, and abilities – not only for the technical aspects of their tasks but also for how to engage effectively as both followers and leaders, if shared leadership is to be optimally effective. Shared leadership also seems more useful in settings where the work is more complex, where the tasks are interdependent, and where people clearly understand their shared goals. We know that if the vertical leader is empowering, and if they display humility, the people who work for them are more likely to share the lead. Yet, these are but a few considerations regarding shared leadership: Shared leadership requires far more research, not only on its outcomes but also on its antecedents, mediators and moderators. As research continues to delve deeper into shared leadership processes, we will yield more insights for the organizations of the future.

A lingering question regarding shared leadership might involve the applicability of shared leadership in divergent cultural circumstances: that is, how does it apply across the globe? Interestingly, multiple empirical studies have investigated shared leadership in such places as China, the Republic of South Korea, Switzerland, Pakistan, Germany, the Netherlands, the United Arab Emirates, Iran, Finland, Denmark, Turkey and Afghanistan. The results are generally consistent – shared leadership appears to be a robust concept which transcends geographic and cultural boundaries. Pearce and Wassenaar (2014) provide an in-depth analysis regarding the cultural factors that both facilitate, as well as discourage, shared leadership (see Table 4). A deeper look into these dimensions, from Hofstede (1980), reveals that most countries have cultural values that both favor and impede

Table 4 Cultural dimensions, definitions, and shared leadership orientations

Cultural Dimension	Definition	Shared Leadership Orientation
Power Distance	High power distance societies are: Authoritarian; Ordered; and Power is centralized	Impediment
	Low Power Distance societies are: Participative; Egalitarian; and Power is dispersed	Facilitator
Aggressiveness-Nurturing	Aggressive societies are: Assertive; Materialistic; and Competitive	Impediment
	Nurturing societies are: Developmental; Encouragement Oriented and Cooperative	Facilitator
Individualism-Collectivism	Individualistic societies are: Self-reliant; Achievement oriented; and Independence oriented	Impediment
	Collectivistic societies are: Group dependent; Relationship oriented; and Loyal to in-groups	Facilitator

Adapted from: Pearce & Wassenaar (2014). Organizational Dynamics

shared leadership (see Table 5). No countries or regions could be characterized as either highly conducive, or lowly conducive to shared leadership: All countries and regions fall into the categories as moderately low or moderately high conducivity to shared leadership. The upshot is that shared leadership is more-or-less universally supported across most societies, but implementing shared leadership requires special attention to the cultural values that are idiosyncratic to the people involved (see Pearce & Osmond, 1996).

As a final thought, we would like to simply remind you that people crave community. We can see this throughout history, in every form of society, and on

Table 5 Cultural orientations and the conducivity to shared leadership

	Individualism Power Distance		Collectivism Power Distance	
	High PD	Low PD	High PD	Low PD
Aggressive	Low Conducivity NA	Moderately Low Conducivity Australia, Canada, Great Britain, India, Ireland, Jamaica, New Zealand, South Africa, Switzerland, USA	Moderately Low Conducivity Arab Countries, Belgium, Columbia, Ecuador, Greece, Hong Kong, Malaysia, Mexico, Pakistan, Philippines, Venezuela	Moderately High Conducivity NA
Nurturing	Moderately Low Conducivity NA	Moderately High Conducivity Argentina, Austria, Denmark, Finland, Germany, Israel, Italy, Japan, Netherlands, Norway, Sweden	Moderately High Conducivity Brazil, Chile, Costa Rica, East Africa, France, Guatemala, Indonesia, Iran, Korea, Panama, Peru, Portugal, El Salvador, Singapore, Spain, Taiwan, Thailand, Turkey, Uruguay, West Africa, Yugoslavia	High Conducivity NA

Adapted from: Pearce & Wassenaar (2014). Organizational Dynamics.

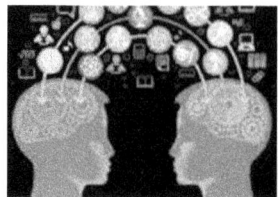

Figure 16 Philosophical perspective on shared leadership

each continent. They have had to decide how they worked together, and history is littered with examples of societies where leadership was shared to various degrees, for countless reasons. But those societies developed organically, and the difference is, we are now given the opportunity to *choose to share the lead,* with intention, knowing what we will all gain – together.

We would like to close with a Nigerian Proverb, which captures the essence of our Element (see Figure 16).

References

Abson, E., & Schofield, P. (2022). Exploring the antecedents of shared leadership in event organisations. *Journal of Hospitality and Tourism Management*, 52, 439–451.

Aguilar, F. (1967). *Scanning the Business Environment*. New York: Macmillan.

Avolio, B. J., Jung, D., Murray, W., & Sivasubramaniam, N. (1996). Building highly developed teams: Focusing on shared leadership process, efficacy, trust, and performance. In M. M. Beyerlein, D. A. Johnson & S. T. Beyerlein (eds.), *Advances in Interdisciplinary Studies of Work Teams* (pp. 173–209). Greenwich, CT: JAI.

Benne, K. D., & Sheats, P. (1948). Functional roles of group members. *Journal of Social Issues*, 4(2), 41–49.

Berger, J., Cohen, B. P., & Zelditch Jr, M. (1972). Status characteristics and social interaction. *American Sociological Review*, 37, 241–255.

Bergman, J. Z., Rentsch, J. R., Small, E. E., Davenport, S. W., & Bergman, S. M. (2012). The shared leadership process in decision-making teams. *The Journal of Social Psychology*, 152(1), 17–42.

Bernard, C. (1938). *The Function of the Executive*. Cambridge, MA: Harvard.

Berson, Y., Waldman, D. A., & Pearce, C. L. (2016). Enhancing our understanding of vision in organizations: Toward an integration of leader and follower processes. *Organizational Psychology Review*, 6(2), 171–191. https://doi.org/10.1177/2041386615583736.

Bligh, M. C. & Pearce, C. L. (2014). Shared leadership in a high growth environment: Realizing the American dream at Panda Restaurant Group. In C. L. Pearce, C. C. Manz, & H. P. Sims (eds.), *Share, Don't Take the Lead* (pp. 147–162). Charlotte, NC: IAP.

Bligh, M. C., Pearce, C. L., & Kohles, J. C. (2006). The importance of self-and shared leadership in team based knowledge work: A meso-level model of leadership dynamics. *Journal of Managerial Psychology*, 21(4), 296–318.

Boies, K., Lvina, E., & Martens, M. L. (2010). Shared leadership and team performance in a business strategy simulation. *Journal of Personnel Psychology*, 9(4), 195–202.

Bono, J., Purvanova, R., Towler, A., & Peterson, D. (2009). A survey of executive coaching practices. *Personnel Psychology*, 62, 361–404.

Bowers, D. G., & Seashore, S. E. (1966). Predicting organizational effectiveness with a four-factor theory of leadership. *Administrative Science Quarterly*, 11(2), 238–263.

Burke, C. S., Fiore, S. M., & Salas, E. (2003). The role of shared cognition in enabling shared leadership and team adaptability. In C. L. Pearce & J. A. Conger (eds.), *Shared Leadership: Reframing the Hows and Whys of Leadership, 103*. Thousand Oaks, CA: Sage.

Cannon-Bowers, J. A., Salas, E., & Converse, S. (1993). Shared mental models in expert team decision making. In N. J. Castellan, Jr. (ed.), *Individual and Group Decision Making: Current Issues* (pp. 221–246). Hillsdale, NJ: Lawrence Erlbaum Associates.

Carson, J. B., Tesluk, P. E., & Marrone, J. A. (2007). Shared leadership in teams: An investigation of antecedent conditions and performance. *Academy of Management Journal, 50*(5), 1217–1234.

Carvalho, J., Sobral, F., & Mansur, J. (2020). Exploring shared leadership in public organizations: evidence from the educational arena. *Revista de Administração Pública, 54*, 524–544.

Castellano, S., Chandavimol, K., Khelladi, I., & Orhan, M. A. (2021). Impact of self-leadership and shared leadership on the performance of virtual R&D teams. *Journal of Business Research, 128*, 578–586.

Chiu, C. Y. (2014). *Investigating the Emergence of Shared Leadership in Teams: The Roles of Team Proactivity, Internal Social Context, and Leader Humility*. Buffalo, NY: State University of New York at Buffalo.

Chiu, C. Y., Owens, B. P., & Tesluk, P. E. (2016). Initiating and utilizing shared leadership in teams: The role of leader humility, team proactive personality, and team performance capability. *Journal of Applied Psychology, 101*(12), 1705–1720.

Choi, S. B., Kim, K., & Kang, S. W. (2017). Effects of transformational and shared leadership styles on employees' perception of team effectiveness. *Social Behavior and Personality: An International Journal, 45*(3), 377–386.

Cohen, S. G., & Bailey, D. E. (1997). What makes teams work: Group effectiveness research from the shop floor to the executive suite. *Journal of Management, 23*, 239–290.

Conger, J. A., & Kanungo, R. N. (1988). The empowerment process: Integrating theory and practice. *Academy of Management Review, 13*, 639–652.

Conger, J. A., & Pearce, C. L. (2003). A landscape of opportunities. In C. L. Pearce & J. A. Conger (eds.), *Shared Leadership: Reframing the Hows and Whys of Leadership* (pp. 285–303). Thousand Oaks, CA: Sage.

Conger, J. A., & Pearce, C. L. (2009). Using empowerment to motivate people to engage in effective self- and shared leadership. In E. A. Locke (ed.), *Principles of Organizational Behavior* (pp. 201–216). New York: John Wiley.

Contractor, N. S., DeChurch, L. A., Carson, J., Carter, D. R., & Keegan, B. (2012). The topology of collective leadership. *The Leadership Quarterly, 23* (6), 994–1011.

Cordery, J., Soo, C., Kirkman, B., Rosen, B., & Mathieu, J. (2009). Leading parallel global virtual teams: Lessons from Alcoa. *Organizational Dynamics, 38*, 204–216.

Coun, M. J., Gelderman, C. J., & Perez-Arendsen, J. (2015). Shared leadership and proactivity in the New Ways of Working. *Gedrag & Organisatie, 28*(4), 356–379.

Coun, M. J. H., Peters, P., & Blomme, R. J. (2019). "Let's share!" The mediating role of employees' self-determination in the relationship between transformational and shared leadership and perceived knowledge sharing among peers. *European Management Journal, 37*, 481–491.

Cox, J. F., Pearce, C. L., & Perry, M. L. (2003). Toward a model of shared leadership and distributed influence in the innovation process. In C. A. Pearce & J. A. Conger (eds.), *Shared Leadership: Reframing the Hows and Whys of Leadership* (pp. 69–102). Thousand Oaks, CA: Sage.

Cox, J. F., Pearce, C. L., & Sims, H. P., Jr. (2003). Toward a broader agenda for leadership development: Extending the traditional transactional–transformational duality by developing directive, empowering and shared leadership skills. In S. E. Murphy & R. E. Riggio (eds.), *The Future of Leadership Development* (pp. 161–180). Mahwah, NJ: Lawrence Erlbaum.

Darban, M. (2022). Learning in virtual student teams: An examination of shared leadership. *Journal of Research on Technology in Education, 54*(5), 736–753.

Daspit, J., Justice Tillman, C., Boyd, N. G., & Mckee, V. (2013). Cross-functional team effectiveness: An examination of internal team environment, shared leadership, and cohesion influences. *Team Performance Management: An International Journal, 19*(1/2), 34–56.

DeRue, D. S., Nahrgang, J. D., & Ashford, S. J. (2015). Interpersonal perceptions and the emergence of leadership structures in groups: A network perspective. *Organization Science, 26*(4), 1192–1209.

Dirks, K. T., & Ferrin, D. L. (2002). Trust in leadership: Meta-analytic findings and implications for research and practice. *Journal of Applied Psychology, 87*, 611–628.

D'Innocenzo, L., Mathieu, J. E., & Kukenberger, M. R. (2014). A meta-analysis of different forms of shared leadership–team performance relations. *Journal of Management, 42*, 1964–1991.

Drescher, M. A., Korsgaard, M. A., Welpe, I. M., Picot, A., & Wigand, R. T. (2014). The dynamics of shared leadership: Building trust and enhancing performance. *Journal of Applied Psychology, 99*(5), 771.

Drescher, G., & Garbers, Y. (2016). Shared leadership and commonality: A policy-capturing study. *The Leadership Quarterly, 27*(2), 200–217.

Drucker, P. F. (1954). *The Practice of Management.* New York: Harper & Row.

Drucker, P. F. (1969). *The age of discontinuity: Guidelines to our changing society.* New York: Harper & Row.

Drucker, P. F. (1995). *Management in Time of Great Change.* New York: Penguin Putnam.

Durkheim, É. (1893). *The Division of Labor in Society.* Glencoe: Free Press.

Durkheim, E. (1895/1938). *The Rules of Sociological Method* (8th ed.). Chicago: University of Chicago Press.

Durkheim, É. (1973). *Emile Durkheim on Morality and Society.* Edited by R. N. Bellah. Chicago: University of Chicago Press.

Elloy, D. F. (2008). The relationship between self-leadership behaviors and organization variables in a self-managed work team environment. *Management Research News, 31*, 801–810.

Ensley, M. D., Hmieleski, K. M., & Pearce, C. L. (2006). The importance of vertical and shared leadership within new venture top management teams: Implications for the performance of startups. *The Leadership Quarterly, 17*, 217–231.

Ensley, M. D., Pearson, A., & Pearce, C. L. (2003). Top management team process, shared leadership, and new venture performance: A theoretical model and research agenda. *Human Resource Management Review, 13*(2), 329–346.

Erez, M., & Arad, R. (1986). Participative goal-setting: Social, motivational, and cognitive factors. *Journal of Applied Psychology, 71*(4), 591–597.

Erkutlu, H. (2012). The impact of organizational culture on the relationship between shared leadership and team proactivity. *Team Performance Management: An International Journal, 18*, 102–119.

Fausing, M. S., Jeppe Jeppesen, H., Jønsson, T. S., Lewandowski, J., & Bligh, M. C. (2013). Moderators of shared leadership: Work function and team autonomy. *Team Performance Management: An International Journal, 19*(5/6), 244–262

Fausing, M. S., Joensson, T. S., Lewandowski, J., & Bligh, M. (2015). Antecedents of shared leadership: Empowering leadership and interdependence. *Leadership & Organization Development Journal, 36*(3), 271–291.

Festinger, L. (1953). Behavior in a level of aspiration situation affected by group comparison. PhD Thesis, University of Minnesota.
Follett, M. P. (1924). *Creative Experience.* New York: Longmans Green.
Fransen, K., Delvaux, E., Mesquita, B., & Van Puyenbroeck, S. (2018). The emergence of shared leadership in newly formed teams with an initial structure of vertical leadership: A longitudinal analysis. *The Journal of Applied Behavioral Science, 54*(2), 140–170.
Galli, B. J., Kaviani, M. A., Bottani, E., & Murino, T. (2017). Shared leadership and key innovation indicators in six sigma projects. *International Journal of Strategic Decision Sciences (IJSDS), 8*(4), 1–45.
Gantt, H. L. (1916). *Industrial Leadership.* New Haven, CT: Yale University Press.
Ge, X., Liu, S., Zhang, Q. et al. (2024). What facilitates the emergence of shared leadership? The predictive role of team personality composition. *Chinese Management Studies, 18*(6), www.emerald.com/insight/1750-614X.htm.
George, V., Burke, L. J., Rodgers, B. et al. (2002). Developing staff nurse shared leadership behavior in professional nursing practice. *Nursing Administration Quarterly, 26*(3), 44–59.
Gilbreth, F. B. (1912). *Primer of Scientific Management.* New York: Van Nostrand Reinhold.
Gilbreth, F. B., & Gilbreth, L. M. (1917). *Applied Motion Study.* New York: Sturgis & Walton.
Graen, G. B. (1976). Role-making processes within complex organizations. In M. D. Dunnette (Ed.), *Handbook of Industrial and Organizational Psychology* (pp. 1201–1245). Chicago: Rand Mc-Nally.
Grille, A., Schulte, E. M., & Kauffeld, S. (2015). Promoting shared leadership: A multilevel analysis investigating the role of prototypical team leader behavior, psychological empowerment, and fair rewards. *Journal of Leadership & Organizational Studies, 22*(3), 324–339.
Gu, J., Chen, Z., Huang, Q., Liu, H., & Huang, S. (2018). A multilevel analysis of the relationship between shared leadership and creativity in inter-organizational teams. *The Journal of Creative Behavior, 52*(2), 109–126.
Gu, Q., Hu, D., & Hempel, P. (2022). Team reward interdependence and team performance: roles of shared leadership and psychological ownership. *Personnel Review, 51*(5), 1518–1533.
Hans, S., & Gupta, R. (2018). Job characteristics affect shared leadership: The moderating effect of psychological safety and perceived self-efficacy. *Leadership & Organization Development Journal, 39*(6), 730–744.
Heenan, D. A., & Bennis, W. G. (1999). *Co-leaders: The Power of Great Partnerships.* New York, NY: John Wiley & Sons.

References

Hess, J. P. (2015). Enabling and sustaining shared leadership in autonomous teams. *European Scientific Journal, 1*, 82–95.

Hmieleski, K. M., Cole, M. S., & Baron, R. A. (2012). Shared authentic leadership and new venture performance. *Journal of Management, 38*, 1476–1499.

Hoch, J. E. (2013). Shared leadership and innovation: The role of vertical leadership and employee integrity. *Journal of Business and Psychology, 28*, 159–174.

Hoch, J. E., & Kozlowski, S. W. (2014). Leading virtual teams: Hierarchical leadership, structural supports, and shared team leadership. *Journal of Applied Psychology, 99*, 390–403.

Hoch, J. E., Pearce, C. L., & Welzel, L. (2010). Is the most effective team leadership shared?. *Journal of Personnel Psychology, 9*(3), 105–116.

Hofstede, G. (1980). *Culture Consequences: International Variations in Organizations*. Beverly Hills, CA: Sage.

Hollander, E. P. (1961). Some effects of perceived status on responses to innovative behavior. *Journal of Abnormal and Social Psychology, 63*, 247–250.

Hollander, E. P. (1978). *Leadership Dynamics: A Practical Guide to Effective Relationships*. New York: Free Press.

Homans, G. C. (1958). Social behavior as exchange. *American Journal of Sociology, 63*, 597–606.

Hooker, C., & Csikszentmihalyi, M. (2003). Flow, creativity, and shared leadership: Rethinking the motivation and structuring of knowledge work. In C. L. Pearce & J. A. Conger (eds.), *Shared Leadership: Reframing the Hows and Whys of Leadership* (pp. 217–234). Thousand Oaks, CA: Sage.

Houghton, J. D., Neck, C. P., & Manz, C. C. (2003). Self-leadership and superleadership. In C. L. Pearce & J. A. Conger (eds.), *Shared Leadership: Reframing the Hows and Whys of Leadership*, (pp. 123–140). Thousand Oaks, CA: Sage.

Kang, S., & Svensson, P. G. (2023). The antecedents of shared leadership in sport for development and peace collaboratives. *Journal of Sport Management, 1*(aop), 1–12.

Karau, S. J., & Williams, K. D. (1993). Social loafing: A meta-analytic review and theoretical integration. *Journal of Personality and Social Psychology, 65*(4), 681.

Karriker, J. H., Madden, L. T., & Katell, L. A. (2017). Team composition, distributed leadership, and performance: It's good to share. *Journal of Leadership & Organizational Studies, 24*(4), 507–518.

Kelly, R. E. (1988). In praise of followers. *Harvard Business Review*, *66*(6), 141–148.

Kerr, S., & Jermier, J. (1978). Substitutes for leadership: Their meaning and measurement. *Organizational Behavior and Human Performance*, *22*, 374–403.

Kidwell Jr, R. E., & Bennett, N. (1993). Employee propensity to withhold effort: A conceptual model to intersect three avenues of research. *Academy of Management Review*, *18*(3), 429–456.

Klasmeier, K. N., & Rowold, J. (2020). A multilevel investigation of predictors and outcomes of shared leadership. *Journal of Organizational Behavior*, *41*(9), 915–930.

Klein, K. J., Ziegert, J. C., Knight, A. P., & Xiao, Y. (2006). Dynamic delegation: Shared, hierarchical, and deindividualized leadership in extreme action teams. *Administrative Science Quarterly*, *51*(4), 590–621.

Klimoski, R., & Mohammed, S. (1994). Team mental model: Construct or metaphor? *Journal of Management*, *20*(2), 403–437.

Konu, A., & Viitanen, E. (2008). Shared leadership in Finnish social and health care. *Leadership in Health Services*, *21*, 28–40.

Kuhn, T. S. (1962). *The Structure of Scientific Revolutions*. Chicago: University of Chicago Press.

Kukenberger, M. R., & D'Innocenzo, L. (2020). The building blocks of shared leadership: The interactive effects of diversity types, team climate, and time. *Personnel Psychology*, *73*(1), 125–150.

Lee, D. S., Lee, K. C., & Seo, Y. W. (2015). An analysis of shared leadership, diversity, and team creativity in an e-learning environment. *Computers in Human Behavior*, *42*, 47–56.

Leonard, H. S., & Goff, M. (2003). Leadership development as an intervention for organizational transformation. *Consulting Psychology Journal*, *55*, 58–67.

Liden, R. C., & Graen, G. (1979, November). The impact of leader-member exchange on job resignation. In *Proceedings of the 11th Annual Meeting of American Institute for Decision Sciences* (pp. 348–350), New Orleans, Louisiana.

Liu, S., Hu, J., Li, Y., Wang, Z., & Lin, X. (2014). Examining the cross-level relationship between shared leadership and learning in teams: Evidence from China. *The Leadership Quarterly*, *25*(2), 282–295.

Lorinkova, N. M., & Bartol, K. M. (2021). Shared leadership development and team performance: A new look at the dynamics of shared leadership. *Personnel Psychology*, *74*(1), 77–107.

Lyndon, S., & Pandey, A. (2020). Shared leadership in entrepreneurial teams: A qualitative study. *Journal of Indian Business Research, 12*(3), 427–441.

Lyndon, S., Pandey, A., & Navare, A. (2022). Emergence and outcomes of shared leadership: Unraveling the role of transactive memory system and team mindfulness using mixed-methods approach. *Leadership & Organization Development Journal, 43*(2), 196–210.

Maier, N. R. (1967). Assets and liabilities in group problem solving: The need for an integrative function. *Psychological Review, 74*(4), 239.

Manz, C. C. (1986). Self-leadership: Toward an expanded theory of self-influence processes in organizations. *Academy of Management Review, 11*(3), 585–600.

Manz, C. C., & Sims, H. P., Jr. (1980). Self-management as a substitute for leadership: A social learning theory perspective. *Academy of Management Review, 5*, 361–367.

Manz, C. C., & Sims Jr, H. P. (1987). Leading workers to lead themselves: The external leadership of self-managing work teams. *Administrative Science Quarterly, 32*, 106–129.

Margolis, J. A., & Ziegert, J. C. (2016). Vertical flow of collectivistic leadership: An examination of the cascade of visionary leadership across levels. *The Leadership Quarterly, 27*(2), 334–348.

Marks, M. A., Mathieu, J. E., & Zaccaro, S. J. 2001. A temporally based framework and taxonomy of team processes. *Academy of Management Review, 26*(3), 356–376.

Mathieu, J. E., Kukenberger, M. R., D'innocenzo, L., & Reilly, G. (2015). Modeling reciprocal team cohesion–performance relationships, as impacted by shared leadership and members' competence. *Journal of Applied Psychology, 100*(3), 713.

Mathieu, J., Maynard, M. T., Rapp, T., & Gilson. L. 2008. Team Effectiveness 1997–2007: A review of recent advancements and a glimpse into the future. *Journal of Management, 34*, 410–476. https://doi.org/10.1177/0149206 308316061

Masal, D. (2015). Shared and transformational leadership in the police. *Policing: An International Journal of Police Strategies & Management, 38*(1), 40–55.

Mayo, E. G. (1933). *The Human Relations Movement*. Boston, MA: Harvard Business School, Historical Collections, Baker Library.

Mayo, M., Meindl, J. R., & Pastor, J. C. (2003). Shared leadership in work teams: A social network approach. In C. L. Pearce & J. A. Conger (eds.), *Shared Leadership: Reframing the Hows and Whys of Leadership*, 193–214. Thousand Oaks, CA: Sage.

McGrath, J. E. (1964). *Social Psychology: A Brief Introduction*. New York: Holt, Rinehart & Winston.

Mehra, A., Smith, B. R., Dixon, A. L., & Robertson, B. (2006). Distributed leadership in teams: The network of leadership perceptions and team performance. *The Leadership Quarterly, 17*(3), 232–245.

Mi, Y., Zhang, X., Liang, L., Tian, G., & Tian, Y. (2024). To share or not to share: How perceived institutional empowerment shapes employee perceived shared leadership. *Current Psychology, 43*(6), 4918–4929.

Mihalache, O. R., Jansen, J. J. P., Bosch, F. A. J. V. D., & Volberda, H. W. (2014). Top management team shared leadership and organizational ambidexterity: A moderated mediation framework. *Strategic Entrepreneurship Journal, 8*, 128–148.

Montgomery, J. (1836). *The Theory and Practice of Cotton Spinning; Or the Carding and Spinning Master's Assistant*. Glasgow, Scotland: John Niven, Trongate.

Montgomery, J. (1840). *The Cotton Manufacture of the United States of America Contrasted and Compared with That of Great Britain*. London: John N. Van.

Muethel, M., Gehrlein, S., & Hoegl, M. (2012). Socio-demographic factors and shared leadership behaviors in dispersed teams: Implications for human resource management. *Human Resource Management, 51*(4), 525–548.

Nardinelli, C., (2008). *Industrial Revolution and the Standard of Living*. Library of Economics and Liberty. www.econlib.org/library/Enc/IndustrialRevolutionandtheStandardofLiving.html.

Nicolaides, V. C., LaPort, K. A., Chen, T. R. et al. (2014). The shared leadership of teams: A meta-analysis of proximal, distal, and moderating relationships. *The Leadership Quarterly, 25*(5), 923–942. https://doi.org/10.1016/j.leaqua.2014.06.006

O'Bannon, Douglas P. & Craig L. Pearce. (1999). A quasi-experiment of gainsharing in service organizations: Implications for organizational citizenship behavior and pay satisfaction. *Journal of Managerial Issues, 11*(3), 363–378.

Olson-Sanders, T. (2006). Collectivity and influence: The nature of shared leadership and its relationship with team learning orientation, vertical leadership and team effectiveness. Doctoral dissertation, George Washington University, 2006. Retrieved from ABI/INFORM Global (Publication No. AAT 3237041).

Paris, L., Howell, J., Dorfman, P., & Hanges, P. (2009). Preferred leadership prototypes of male and female leaders in 27 countries. *Journal of International Business Studies, 40*, 1396–1405.

Paunova, M., & Lee, Y. T. (2016). Collective global leadership in self-managed multicultural teams: The role of team goal orientation. In J. S. Osland, M. Li, M. E. Mendenhall (eds.), *Advances in Global Leadership* (pp. 187–210). Leeds, UK: Emerald Group.

Pearce, C. L. (1993). The Obliteration of Traditional Management. Presented to the Annual Conference of the Association of Management, Atlanta.

Pearce, C. L. (1995). The Determinants of Change Management Team Effectiveness: A Longitudinal Investigation. Presented to the Annual University of Maryland Graduate Research Interaction Day Conference, College Park, Maryland, March, 1995.

Pearce, C. L. (1997). *The Determinants of Change Management Team (CMT) Effectiveness: A Longitudinal Investigation*. Unpublished doctoral dissertation, University of Maryland, College Park.

Pearce, C. L. (2004). The future of leadership: Combining vertical and shared leadership to transform knowledge work. *Academy of Management Executive*, *18*(1), 47–57.

Pearce, C. L. (2010). Leading knowledge workers. In C. L. Pearce, J. A. Macieriello, & H. Yamawaki (eds.), *The Drucker Difference* (pp. 35–45). New York: McGraw-Hill.

Pearce, C. L. (2014). The sky is the limit for shared leadership at Southwest Airlines. In C. L., Pearce, C. C. Manz, & H. P. Sims (eds.), *Share, Don't Take the Lead*. (pp. 51–70). Charlotte, NC: IAP.

Pearce, C. L. (2015). Developmental health services leadership: Integrating hierarchical and shared leadership for health services organizational learning. *Health Services Management Research*, *28*(3–4), 76–82.

Pearce, C. L., & Conger, J. A. (2003). *Shared Leadership: Reframing the Hows and Whys of Leadership*. Thousand Oaks, CA: Sage.

Pearce, C. L., & Ensley, M. D. (2004). A reciprocal and longitudinal investigation of the innovation process: The central role of shared vision in product and process innovation teams (PPITs). *Journal of Organizational Behavior*, *25*(2), 259–278.

Pearce, C. L., Houghton, J. D., Manz, C. C. et al. (2023). Time for a group hug? Toward a theory of shared emotional leadership in and of family business. *Journal of Family Business Strategy*, *14*(2), 100549.

Pearce, C. L., & Jay, A. C. (eds.) (2003). *Shared Leadership: Reframing the Hows and Whys Leadership*. Thousand Oaks, CA: Sage.

Pearce, C. L., & Manz, C. C. (2014). The leadership disease ... and its potential cures. *Business Horizons*, *57*(2), 215–224.

Pearce, C. L., Manz, C. C., & Sims, H. P., Jr. (2014). *Share, Don't Take, the Lead*. Charlotte, NC: Information Age.

References

Pearce, C. L., & Osmond, C. P. (1996). Metaphors for change: The ALPs model of change management. *Organizational Dynamics, 24*(3), 23–35.

Pearce, C. L., & Sims, H. P., Jr. (2000). Shared leadership: Toward a multi-level theory of leadership. In M. M. Beyerlein, D. A. Johnson, & S. T. Beyerlein (eds.), *Advances in Interdisciplinary Studies of Work Teams* (pp. 115–139). Greenwich, CT: JAI.

Pearce, C. L., & Sims, H. P., Jr. (2002). Vertical versus shared leadership as predictors of the effectiveness of change management teams: An examination of aversive, directive, transactional, transformational, and empowering leader behaviors. *Group Dynamics, Theory, Research, and Practice, 6,* 172–197.

Pearce, C. L., Sims, H. P., Cox, J. F. et al. (2003). Transactors, transformers and beyond: A multi-method development of a theoretical typology of leadership. *Journal of Management Development, 22*(4), 273–307.

Pearce, C. L., van Knippenberg, D., & van Ginkel, W. P. (2023). The trouble with teams ... and team leadership: Toward a research agenda on the paradoxical nature and reciprocal dynamics of vertical and shared leadership. *Academy of Management Collections, 2*(3), 31–44.

Pearce, C. L., & Wassenaar, C. L. (2014). Leadership is like fine wine: It is meant to be shared, globally. *Organizational Dynamics, 43,* 9–16.

Pearce, C. L., Wassenaar, C. L., & Manz, C. C. (2014). Is shared leadership the key to responsible leadership? *Academy of Management Perspectives, 28*(3), 275–288.

Pearce, C. L., & van Knippenberg, D. (2024). Moderated paradoxical leadership: Resolving the innovation team leadership conundrum. *Journal of Product Innovation Management, 41*(1), 3–11.

Pearce, C. L., van Knippenberg, D., & Kirchhoff, C. J. (2024). The civil engineering leadership Dilemma: Is calibrated paradoxical leadership the answer? *Journal of Management in Engineering, 40*(3), 02524001.

Pearce, C. L., & van Knippenberg, D. (2023). Social innovation is a team sport: Combining top-down and shared leadership for social innovation. *Business & Society, 63*(5), 00076503231190835.

Pearce, C. L., van Knippenberg, D., & van Ginkel, W. P. (2023). The trouble with teams ... and team leadership: Toward a research agenda on the paradoxical nature and reciprocal dynamics of vertical and shared leadership. *Academy of Management Collections, 2*(3), 31–44.

Pearce, C. L., Wassenaar, C. L., Berson, Y., & Tuval-Mashiach, R. (2019). Toward a theory of meta-paradoxical leadership. *Organizational Behavior and Human Decision Processes, 155,* 31–41.

References

Pearce, C. L., & van Knippenberg, D. (2024). Moderated paradoxical leadership: Resolving the innovation team leadership conundrum. *Journal of Product Innovation Management*, *41*(1), 3–11.

Pearce, C. L., van Knippenberg, D., & Kirchhoff, C. J. (2024). The civil engineering leadership Dilemma: Is calibrated paradoxical leadership the answer? *Journal of Management in Engineering*, *40*(3), 02524001.

Pearce, C. L., van Knippenberg, D., & van Ginkel, W. P. (2023). The trouble with teams … and team leadership: Toward a research agenda on the paradoxical nature and reciprocal dynamics of vertical and shared leadership. *Academy of Management Collections*, *2*(3), 31–44.

Pearce, C. L., Wassenaar, C. L., Berson, Y., & Tuval-Mashiach, R. (2019). Toward a theory of meta-paradoxical leadership. *Organizational Behavior and Human Decision Processes*, *155*, 31–41.

Peter, T., Braun, S., & Frey, D. (2015). How shared leadership affects individual creativity and support for innovation. In *Academy of Management Proceedings* (Vol. 2015, No. 1, p. 16212). Briarcliff Manor, NY 10510: Academy of Management.

Raelin, J. (2006). Does action learning promote collaborative leadership? *Academy of Management Learning & Education*, *5*(2), 152–168.

Ropo, A., & Sauer, E. (2003). Partnerships of orchestras: Towards shared leadership. *International Journal of Arts Management*, *5*(2), 44–55.

Rose, R., Groeger, L., & Hölzle, K. (2021). The emergence of shared leadership in innovation labs. *Frontiers in Psychology*, *12*, 685167.

Rousseau, J. J. (2018). *Rousseau: The Social Contract and Other Later Political Writings*. Cambridge, UK: Cambridge University Press.

Say, J. B. (1803/1964). *A Treatise on Political Economy*. New York: Augustus M. Kelley. (Original work published 1803).

Seers, A. (1989). Team-member exchange quality: A new construct for role-making research. *Organizational Behavior and Human Decision Processes*, *43*(1), 118–135.

Seibert, S. E., Sparrowe, R. T., & Liden, R. C. (2003). A group exchange structure approach to leadership in groups. In C. L. Pearce & J. A. Conger (eds.), *Shared Leadership: Reframing the Hows and Whys of Leadership*, 173–192. Thousand Oaks, CA: Sage.

Serban, A., & Roberts, A. J. (2016). Exploring antecedents and outcomes of shared leadership in a creative context: A mixed-methods approach. *The Leadership Quarterly*, *27*(2), 181–199.

Shamir, B., & Lapidot, Y. (2003). Shared leadership in the management of group boundaries: A study of expulsions from officers' training courses. In

C. L. Pearce & J. A. Conger (eds.), *Shared Leadership: Reframing the Hows and Whys of Leadership* (pp. 235–249). Thousand Oaks, CA: Sage.

Shaw, M. E. (1981). *Team Dynamics: The Psychology of Small Team Behavior.* New York: McGra-Hill.

Siangchokyoo, N., & Klinger, R. L. (2022). Shared leadership and team performance: The joint effect of team dispositional composition and collective identification. *Group & Organization Management, 47*(1), 109–140.

Solomon, A., Loeffler, F. J., & Frank, G. H. (1953). An analysis of co-therapist interaction in group psychotherapy. *International Journal of Group Psychotherapy, 3*, 171–180.

Strauss, A., & Corbin, J. (1998). *Basics of Qualitative Research Techniques* (2nd ed.). Thousand Oaks, CA: Sage.

Stewart, L. (1998). A meaning for machines: Modernity, utility, and the eighteenth century British public. *Journal of Modern History, 70*, 259–294.

Stewart, L. (2003). Science and the eighteenth-century public: Scientific revolutions and the changing format of scientific investigation. In M. Fitzpatrick, P. Jones, C. Knelworf, & I. McAlmon (eds.), *The Enlightenment World* (pp. 234–246). London: Routledge.

Svensson, P. G., Jones, G. J., & Kang, S. (2021). The influence of servant leadership on shared leadership development in sport for development. *Journal of Sport Development, 10*, 17–24.

Taylor, F. W. (1903). *Shop Management.* New York: Harper & Row.

Taylor, F. W. (1911). *Principles of Scientific Management.* New York: Harper & Brothers.

Tung, Y. C., & Shih, C. T. (2023). To lead or not? The role theory perspective on the moderating roles of transformational and laissez-faire leadership in shared leadership teams. *Asia Pacific Journal of Management*, 1–28.

Turner, C. E. (1933). Test room studies in employee effectiveness. *American Journal of Public Health and the Nation's Health, 23*(6), 577–584.

Van Knippenberg, D., Pearce, C. L., & van Ginkel, W. (2024). Shared leadership—vertical leadership dynamics in teams. (working paper).

Van Knippenberg, D., & Sitkin, S. B. (2013). A critical assessment of charismatic—transformational leadership research: Back to the drawing board? *The Academy of Management Annals, 7*(1), 1–60.

Vandavasi, R. K. K., McConville, D. C., Uen, J. F., & Yepuru, P. (2020). Knowledge sharing, shared leadership and innovative behaviour: A cross-level analysis. *International Journal of Manpower, 41*(8), 1221–1233.

Van Zyl, J. (2020). *Leadership Behaviour that Facilitate Shared Leadership Emergence in Internationally Dispersed Non-Formal Teams.* Doctoral dissertation, University of Pretoria.

Von Stieglitz, S. K. (2023). *Antecedents to Shared Leadership in Virtual Teams.* Doctoral dissertation, Macquarie University.

Vroom, V. H., & Yetton, P. W. (1973). *Leadership and Decision-Making* (Vol. 110). Pittsburgh, PA: University of Pittsburgh Press.

Wang, D., Waldman, D. A., & Zhang, Z. (2014). A meta-analysis of shared leadership and team effectiveness. *Journal of Applied Psychology, 99*(2), 181.

Wang, L., Han, J., Fisher, C. M., & Pan, Y. (2017). Learning to share: Exploring temporality in shared leadership and team learning. *Small Group Research, 48*(2), 165–189.

Wang, L., Jiang, W., Liu, Z., & Ma, X. (2017). Shared leadership and team effectiveness: The examination of LMX differentiation and servant leadership on the emergence and consequences of shared leadership. *Human Performance, 30*(4), 155–168.

Wang, D., Waldman, D. A., & Zhang, Z. (2014). A meta-analysis of shared leadership and team effectiveness. *Journal of Applied Psychology, 99*(2), 181.

Wassenaar, C. L. (2017). *What Makes Leadership Shared? Test of a Mediational Model.* Doctoral dissertation, The Claremont Graduate University.

Wassenaar, C. L. & Pearce, C. L. (2012). The nature of shared leadership. In D. V. Day & J. Antonakis (eds), *The Nature of Leadership*, 2nd ed. (pp. 363–389). Thousand Oaks, CA: Sage.

Wassenaar, C. L., Pearce, C. L., Hoch, J., & Wegge, J. (2010). Shared leadership meets virtual teams: A match made in cyberspace. In P. Yoong (ed.), *Leadership in the Digital Enterprise: Issues and Challenges* (pp. 15–27). Hersey, PA: IGI Global.

West, M. A. (ed.) (1996). Reflexivity and work group effectiveness: A conceptual integration. In *Handbook of Work Group Psychology* (pp. 555–579). Thousand Oaks, CA: Sage.

Wood, M. S. (2005). Determinants of shared leadership in management teams. *International Journal of Leadership Studies, 1*(1), 64–85.

Wren, D. A. (1994). *The Evolution of Management Thought* (4th ed.). New York: John Wiley.

Wu, Q., & Cormican, K. (2021). Shared leadership and team effectiveness: An investigation of whether and when in engineering design teams. *Frontiers in Psychology, 11*, 4045.

Wu, Q., Cormican, K., & Chen, G. (2020). A meta-analysis of shared leadership: Antecedents, consequences, and moderators. *Journal of Leadership & Organizational Studies, 27*(1), 49–64.

Wu, Q., Zhou, Q., & Cormican, K. (2023). Promoting shared leadership in Lean Six Sigma project teams: Toward a three-way interaction model. *International Journal of Lean Six Sigma, 5*(3), 642–663.

Xu, C., & Zhao, L. (2023). Collective achievement, cohesive support, complementary expertise: 3Cs emergent model for shared leadership. *Human Resource Development International, 26*(2), 175–200.

Zhu, J., Liao, Z., Yam, K. C., & Johnson, R. E. (2018). Shared leadership: A state-of-the-art review and future research agenda. *Journal of Organizational Behavior, 39*(7), 834–852.

Cambridge Elements ≡

Leadership

Series Editors
Ronald E. Riggio
Claremont McKenna College

Ronald E. Riggio, Ph.D., is the Henry R. Kravis Professor of Leadership and Organisational Psychology and former Director of the Kravis Leadership Institute at Claremont McKenna College. Dr. Riggio is a psychologist and leadership scholar with over a dozen authored or edited books and more than 150 articles/book chapters. He has worked as a consultant and serves on multiple editorial boards.

Susan E. Murphy
University of Edinburgh

Susan E. Murphy is Chair in Leadership Development at the University of Edinburgh Business School. She has published numerous articles and book chapters on leadership, leadership development, and mentoring. Susan was formerly Director of the School of Strategic Leadership Studies at James Madison University and Professor of Leadership Studies. Prior to that, she served as faculty and associate director of the Henry R. Kravis Leadership Institute at Claremont McKenna College. She also serves on the editorial board of The Leadership Quarterly.

Founding Editor
† Georgia Sorenson
University of Cambridge

The late Georgia Sorenson, Ph.D., was the James MacGregor Burns Leadership Scholar at the Moller Institute and Moller By-Fellow of Churchill College at Cambridge University. Before coming to Cambridge, she founded the James MacGregor Burns Academy of Leadership at the University of Maryland, where she was Distinguished Research Professor. An architect of the leadership studies field, Dr. Sorenson has authored numerous books and refereed journal articles.

Editorial Advisory Board
Neal M. Ashkanasy, *University of Queensland*
Roya Ayman, *Illinois Institute of Technology*
Kristin Bezio, *University of Richmond*
Richard Boyatzis, *Case Western Reserve University*
Cynthia Cherrey, *International Leadership Association*
Joanne Ciulla, *Rutgers Business School*
Barbara Crosby, *University of Minnesota*
Suzanna Fitzpatrick, *University of Maryland Medical Center*
Al Goethals, *University of Richmond*
Nathan Harter, *Christopher Newport University*
Ali Jones, *Coventry University*
Ronit Kark, *Bar-Ilan University*
Kevin Lowe, *University of Sydney*
Robin Martin, *University of Manchester*

Stella Nkomo, *University of Pretoria*
Rajnandini Pillai, *California State University, San Marcos*
Micha Popper, *University of Haifa*
Terry Price, *University of Richmond*
Krish Raval, *University of Oxford*
Roni Reiter-Palmon, *University of Nebraska*
Birgit Schyns, *Durham University*
Gillian Secrett, *University of Cambridge*
Nicholas Warner, *Claremont McKenna College*

in partnership with

Møller Centre, Churchill College
www.mollercentre.co.uk

The Møller Institute (www.mollerinstitute.com), home of the James McGregor Burns Academy of Leadership, brings together business and academia for practical leadership development and executive education. As part of Churchill College in the University of Cambridge, the Institute's purpose is to inspire individuals to be the best they can be, to accelerate the performance of the organizations which they serve, and, through our work, to covenant profits to Churchill College to support the education of future leaders. In everything we do our focus is to create a positive impact for people, society, and the Environment.

International Leadership Association
www.ila-net.org

The International Leadership Association (www.ila-net.org) is the organization for connecting leadership scholars, practitioners, and educators in ways that serve to enhance their learning, their understanding, and their impact in the world. These exchanges are professionally enriching, serve to elevate the field of leadership, and advance our mission to advance leadership knowledge and practice for a better world.

About the Series

Cambridge Elements in Leadership is multi- and inter-disciplinary, and will have broad appeal for leadership courses in Schools of Business, Education, Engineering, Public Policy, and in the Social Sciences and Humanities. In addition to the scholarly audience, Elements appeals to professionals involved in leadership development and training.

The series is published in partnership with the International Leadership Association (ILA) and the Møller Institute, Churchill College in the University of Cambridge.

Cambridge Elements

Leadership

Elements in the Series

Leadership Studies and the Desire for Shared Agreement: A Narrative Inquiry
Stan Amaladas

Leading the Future of Technology: The Vital Role of Accessible Technologies
Rebecca LaForgia

Cultural Dynamics and Leadership: An Interpretive Approach
Nathan W. Harter

There Is More than One Way to Lead: The Charismatic, Ideological, and Pragmatic (CIP) Theory of Leadership
Samuel T. Hunter and Jeffrey B. Lovelace

Leading for Innovation: Leadership Actions to Enhance Follower Creativity
Michael D Mumford, Tanner R. Newbold, Mark Fichtel and Samantha England

The Hazards of Great Leadership: Detrimental Consequences of Leader Exceptionalism
James K. Beggan, Scott T. Allison and George R. Goethals

The Gift of Transformative Leaders
Nathan O. Hatch

Ethical Leadership in Conflict and Crisis: Evidence from Leaders on How to Make More Peaceful, Sustainable, and Profitable Communities
Jason Miklian and John E. Katsos

Questioning Leadership
Michael Harvey

Peace Leadership: A Story of Peace Dwelling
Stan Amaladas

Network Leadership: Promoting a Healthier World through the Power of Networks
Jeffrey Beeson

Shared Leadership 2.0: Taking Stock and Looking Forward
Christina L. Wassenaar, Craig L. Pearce and Natalia Lorinkova

A full series listing is available at: www.cambridge.org/CELE

For EU product safety concerns, contact us at Calle de José Abascal, 56–1°, 28003 Madrid, Spain or eugpsr@cambridge.org.

www.ingramcontent.com/pod-product-compliance
Lightning Source LLC
LaVergne TN
LVHW020350260326
834688LV00045B/1636